The Catalyst Nurse

The Catalyst Nurse

SYLVIA LAWRENCE

Text Sylvia Fayers Morrissey and Angela Hindle, on behalf of StoryTerrace
Copyright © Sylvia Lawrence

First print November 2023

I would like to thank Keith my husband, for his support, Richard my nephew, for his encouragement, and Angela, who helped me to tell my story.

After my shocking experience of witnessing how some elderly people are cared for, I wish to dedicate the profits from this book to those concerned with caring for the elderly.

CONTENTS

PROLOGUE	11
1. IN THE BEGINNING	13
2. POM PREJUDICE	21
3. GIVING UP THE GOOD TO AIM FOR THE GREAT	27
4. THE ROLLERCOASTER OF EMOTIONS	37
5. RISING ABOVE THE STORM TO FIND THE SUNLIGHT	49
6. A MARRIAGE NOT MADE IN HEAVEN	57
7. FROM BAD TO WORSE	63
8. A POT OF GOLD AT THE END OF A RAINBOW	73
9. LIFE OUTSIDE WORK	81
10. THE KEY OF ADAPTABILITY	87
11. REPORTING BACK ON THE WAY	91

FORWARD

12. THE FALL	97
13. DECISIONS WHICH SHAPE DESTINY	103
14. SHOCKING SCHEMES	109
15. WHAT NEXT?	113
16. DESOLATION	117
17. THE UNTROD SNOW OF THE FUTURE	123
18. WAKING UP TIRED	129
19. THINGS GO ON AND ON	135
20. FINDING THE WILL TO FIND THE WAY	141
21. TRAUMA	151
22. MORE MUDDLES	159
23. MAIL BOX FULL	165
24. THE ONLY WAY IS UP	169
25. WELCOME HOME	175

26. THE FULL STOP   189

EPILOGUE   197

PROLOGUE

Slim, good-looking, displaying an air of arrogance which some thought added to his attractiveness, my husband, Tom, sat in the publisher's office in the seaside town of Torquay. His immaculate suit with matching accessories supported the impression that he was a man of importance. He was on a mission to sell my story of how I had been wronged. He had a thirst for financial gain, whereas I wanted social justice.

Our life was falling apart around us. I had been devastated by all I had experienced and was disappointed in the church. Tom had resigned from an excellent sales position due to my desire to return to England from New Zealand, the land of our dreams.

All the pieces of this jigsaw will slot into place as I now find the strength to relate my story in the way and time I want and in a time and place not dictated by Tom. Protecting the identity of others, I have renamed us all, choosing to call myself Sue as I share how I became a voice in the wilderness when I tried to help the elderly residents of the care home that stole my soul.

The catalyst nurse.

1. IN THE BEGINNING

It seems like a dream when I look back over four decades to the ten happy years of Cornish life at Carlyon Bay, where I had enjoyed a successful four-year career as a district nursing sister and midwife. A sense of adventure had eventually summoned Tom and I to leave our Cornish security and emigrate to New Zealand, which seemed to offer the opportunities we were looking for, having heard so many positive things from my dad's time there.

Tempus fugit and, as I now relate my story, I will take you back to the early 1980s when we felt it was the right decision for me to accept a midwife position in Christchurch. As we sailed out on the QE2, we felt nothing but positivity about our new life. Tom was happy, as always, to feel in control as he booked the crossing and then arranged the road safari across the north of New Zealand down to the south. We soon settled into our luxurious, large three-bedroomed bungalow in Riccarton.

Occasionally, I would feel a sense of disquiet, as if I were a puppet and Tom pulled the strings. However, I was happy in my new position. In his greater wisdom, Tom felt I was overqualified and too experienced for my role, and he insisted I apply for the position he had found of principal nurse for the local church home.

Tom had decreed that this job was just up my street. He listed my qualities as caring and capable; it was difficult not to feel patronised. However, I felt confident enough to attend the interview that Tom had initiated, and I was excited by the prospect of furthering my career. The hospital and home I was applying to work in were owned by the church, which I felt comfortable about, being a practising Christian.

I had chosen my wardrobe in England, and I soon realised fashion wasn't the only thing that was different in New Zealand. Dressed in my blue two-piece suit, I went to meet the church administrator, Neil, who had decided to give me a whistle-stop tour of the establishments I would be working in if I accepted the job. I didn't like the way my Christian name was used as he introduced himself to me; I was much more used to the more formal approach of the English system where I was called 'Sister'.

Neil's insincere smile did nothing to reassure me that this was going to be the job for me. I could sense his rushed style as he ushered me into his Morris Oxford car. He quickly parked up after the 15-minute ride, during which I had tried to engage him in conversation about my views on elderly care. He rapidly jumped out and clearly expected me to follow. It was obvious that this was going to be a brisk tour of one of the church homes, Eden House. Everything was hurry, hurry, hurry!

Neil announced that 60 residents lived in Eden House, indicating by his abrupt attitude that he saw residents as numbers, not as people. As he led me through the dimly lit corridor, I was not impressed by the decor that greeted me –

ageing rose-pink floral wallpaper. Further soulless corridors tried their best to welcome us as I stared at the darkened green walls. I was told, understandably, that patients occupying the rooms wouldn't want to be disturbed at this time of night, but I could not help but wonder why our tour was taking place at such an inappropriate hour.

Nothing spectacular shone out at me, just a worn, tired ambience that surrounded us as we dashed on. I admit I still wasn't in my comfort zone with the continued casual approach. We added to our tour with a visit to Eden Hospital, where a one-storey building from the 1960s stared at me, its many windows shaded in the failing light of twilight. However, I was still able to distinguish the neat garden, which was heart-warming – some sort of order was what I needed to see.

I found it difficult to keep up with Neil's brusque march. He casually waved his hands at the collection of walking aids. I gagged at the smell of urine as I stared into the day room. Neil's agitated voice urged me to move on: time was of the essence. We looked in on the 36 patients who had been bedded for the night in the eight-bed wards. It all felt very mechanical: two nurses attended to a patient, but my request to chat with them was dismissed with what had become Neil's mantra – 'They won't want to be disturbed at this time of night.'

'Time is marching on' were not the harsh words I wanted to hear; they just emitted to me the message that these patients were burdens. I wanted to speak with their carers. I had many questions, but there was always an excuse from

Neil as to why I couldn't explore beyond these endless, darkened corridors.

Our marathon continued as Neil raced me in his car to Hardwick Courts. On the journey, I was fed garbled information about the management structure of the Christian social services. Neil emphasised that they only employed staff who genuinely cared about the elderly, but I already doubted that this organisation practised what they preached.

I was surprised to hear that they had appointed a newly qualified nurse as matron. I soon learnt from Neil's reaction that I was meant to keep my thoughts and comments to myself. I began to question the point of this tour as Neil continued with the same instructions that we couldn't speak to any patients or staff due to the time of night. He was beginning to sound like a parrot with his repetitive reasons why I could never meet and speak to patients or staff. He might as well have shown me a hall of mannequins.

On my return home, post-10 p.m., Tom wanted to know my thoughts on how things had gone. I did not want to add any weight to my resident control freak's attempt to influence me any further, so I kept my cards close to my chest as I replied that my eyes had certainly been opened. I needed time to gather my own thoughts and reflect on them. I gave my attention to Bobbie, our adopted West Highland terrier, ignoring the stares of my husband, who was trying to get me to speak.

Leaving party from staff at Cornwall surgery, 1983.

Family leaving party, 1983.

Apple Tree Lane, Carlyon Bay, the house we sold to move to New Zealand.

2. POM PREJUDICE

Feeling overwhelmed, I sat by the fire, studying the job description folder. I waded through pages containing the required qualifications, details of responsibilities and functions, names of staff and personnel, information on environmental control, conditions, salary, holiday allowance and sick leave.

A walk with Bobbie offered the mental release I needed from such a detailed read. It relieved some of my stress so that on my return home, I felt able to discuss the advantages and disadvantages of the job with prying Tom. I was aware, yet again, of the different approach my husband and I had to life and the way we viewed things. All his comments reminded me that his aim was for me to earn a higher salary, to work more regular hours and to ensure that we had our weekends together. On the other hand, I was tempted by the challenges the job would provide. I knew I would value having the authority to make decisions, and I was keen to have the opportunity to improve patient care. After all, the majority of the residents were Poms. It would be exciting and interesting to discover the New Zealand approach to nursing and elderly social care.

My decision was made, and the following morning, Neil received my phone call to say I would accept the job. I had to give a month's notice from my job in the maternity service.

THE CATALYST NURSE

We had chosen New Zealand after hearing so many positive reports, but I hadn't often felt accepted or that I fitted in with their informal ways. I experienced discrimination as a Pom on several occasions. The porter at the maternity unit always appeared to get pleasure from by throwing the same greeting at me each morning as I arrived in reception: 'The only good Pom is the one that goes home and takes two Dutchies with them.' I had come to realise that the New Zealanders did not like the Dutch either!

Then, there was an evening when I was on the way to my night shift at the maternity unit and spotted a highway patrol car closing in behind me. Unlike the situation in the UK, the highway patrol officers dealt with traffic concerns, as they were a separate organisation from the police. They appeared to be following me even as I turned at the roundabout. The short twilight gave way to darkening skies. I knew I had not been speeding, but the car continued to follow me onto Highway 73. The light traffic meant the car had no need to trail behind me, always maintaining the same distance. I had heard various stories about the bullying tactics of the highway patrol, so my stomach tightened when their blue lights began to flash. I had to pull up by the curb, but they had put their headlights on full, so they blinded me from behind.

As I wound the window down, the stern male voice ordered me to move onto the grass verge as, apparently, I was obstructing the highway. Further instructions were hurled at me by the harsh voice, such as 'Shut off the engine.'

A torch was shone in my face, blinding me to the man's features. He demanded to know who I was and where I was going. I was shaking and feeling dizzy as I managed to tell him that I was a British midwife on my way to my duty. The horrible man mocked me, imitating my accent as he fell to his knees, howling with laughter. 'She's a British midwife working at Burwood.'

He then pulled himself up and took on a softer manner as he spoke at my driver's door, admitting they had just wanted to scare the pants off me – they had certainly done that! Suddenly, my anger and authority returned to me, and I jumped out and stood in front of the highway patrol officer. I noticed the torch he had dropped on the ground, and I picked it up and marched over to his patrol car, where his sidekick sat, wiping away his tears of laughter. I threw it through the open window as I told him to take his toys home with him. I ordered them both to go and do some proper work.

I arrived at the maternity unit and marched past the porter as his usual greeting bounced off me. I strode into the nurses office, and everyone wondered why I was late, a totally out-of-character trait for me. As they heard my story, some colleagues showed little interest, whereas others looked concerned.

The following morning, when my shift ended, I decided to follow the advice of the daytime manager and go to the highway patrol office in Christchurch to report my traumatic experience.

The officer I met there simply smirked as he heard my story before dissolving into laughter. He explained he'd already heard the story from the guys in the car, and they had thought it even more hilarious when I reacted so angrily to them. He also mimicked my accent as I stormed out, full of disgust.

The experience left me more determined than ever to be proud of my nationality and to speak up for what I believed in, ensuring equality for all, regardless of their background.

The QEII, which we sailed on to New Zealand.

Evening on QEII, 1983.

3. GIVING UP THE GOOD TO AIM FOR THE GREAT

I was presented with some placemats and a card as I left my post at the maternity unit. Feelings of sadness engulfed me when my colleagues personally said their farewells – they had been good company and supportive workmates. I felt a little anxious as to whether I had made the right decision to leave this secure post where I was able to fulfil my job description to an excellent standard. My superior, D H Bashford, had kindly given me a copy of my reference for the new position, and I choked with emotion when reading her final, uplifting paragraph:

Sister Lawrence is a very experienced and excellent midwife and shows maturity and judgement not often seen. She also has a relaxed and informal, reassuring manner with the patients and staff. We will be sorry to lose her as a midwife in New Zealand, and I have no hesitation in recommending her to any position for which she applies.

I understood that I would never know where I was going if I allowed myself to keep looking back, so I set my mind on the present and slipped on my smart navy spotted dress with its white collar and cuffs. Feeling the part, I was ready to start my new career. I told myself that, yes, I had given up a good job, but I was going to make a great difference in the lives of so many residents through this new post.

I felt confident as I pushed open the front door of Church House, holding my head high as I searched out the administrator's office, which bore the nameplate of Pat Moss.

Pat's professional and kind welcome made me feel relaxed. Over a pot of tea, she explained she would arrange an orientation tour for me where I would have the opportunity to ask any questions. Her English accent was a comfort in this new environment, and on hearing that she had emigrated from Gloucester 20 years previously, I dared to hope this was a sign that I was soon going to feel at home in my new job.

Pat explained moving to New Zealand meant she and her husband had accepted lesser careers. Back in England, she had worked for the Ministry of Defence, and her husband, who now made a living by chopping logs, had been a highly skilled cabinet maker. However, they felt the decision to emigrate had been worth it because their children had gained excellent qualifications, entering careers they felt would have been out of their reach back in England.

I felt happy in Pat's company – she reminded me of a mother hen fussing over me as we walked around the offices. I took care not to slip on the polished floors, impressed by the obviously high standards of cleanliness. In one office, I was introduced to several people whose names I tried to register: Jim Stuck, the personnel officer, and Barbara Lewis, a contracted coordinator. I was told that my main points of contact would be Barbara and the man I was to report to, called Patrick. With joy in my step I turned to follow the others out as our gathering dispersed, but Jim pulled me back by my hand, whispering, 'My lunch is 1–2 and my office door is unlocked. If you want to look through the staff files, you'll find them in the top drawer of my filing cabinet.'

What was I to make of that unexpected and unusual interaction? Lost for words, I hoped my smile would suffice as I rushed to catch up with the others.

During the meeting with Patrick, it was like music to my ears when he informed me I was to have an office created for me at Eden House, and he would appreciate regular morning meetings. I welcomed the idea of such an organised start to my daily routine, daring to believe Tom had been right to make me aware of this new career.

Driving home that first night, my thoughts were a jumble: there had been many promising moments of my day, and I tried to ignore the alarm bells of a few things I had noticed, telling myself not to be paranoid and suspicious.

A sickly smell of fat accosted me as I pushed open the door and tried not to gag at the whiff of frying bacon – a cooked breakfast, at this time of early evening, was not really what I fancied. However, the look of pride on Tom's face as he dished it up reminded me to be grateful for this token of support as he eagerly awaited the news from my first day. I was on a high anyway, so I enjoyed enthusing about the vases of sweet-smelling flowers, the immaculate offices and the planned daily pre-shift chat with Patrick. Life was feeling good.

Tom was satisfied with my report back – he liked it when things went to plan – and he then regaled me with the occurrences of his day in Christchurch, where he had been dealing with the shipment of our furniture from England and our Nissan Cherry, which would stand out with its sporty design on the roads of New Zealand. Apparently, the environment office was keen to ensure that our gardening equipment had no bacteria that could be introduced into the country.

My 'Mr Think Ahead' had even found hours in the day to secure himself an interview for a job as a sales representative with Stick Fast. Hubby had certainly got the manipulative skills needed for the post, so I knew without a doubt that the job would be his.

'Let's celebrate our successful day by taking Bobbie for a walk,' I suggested, jumping up for his lead. I had to use up some of those calories supplied by Tom's massive meal!

I jumped out of bed the following morning, full of the joys of our new life – we certainly seemed to have made a wise decision by moving here. I couldn't wait to plunge into my day's work. Wearing my rose-tinted spectacles, I set off for work, noticing how even the roads here were superior: not a pothole in sight! I wondered whether the staff nurse had been joking or if it was really true that, in some areas, cars could drive on the train lines.

Arriving at Church House, I was delighted to see Patrick had fulfilled my expectations: he was prompt and waiting for our appointment. The grandeur of his office decor added a professional ambience to our meetings. I sat in a mahogany seat across from the vintage desk where Patrick sat in his green gilded chair, complemented so well by the gold-papered walls.

He professionally commenced our meeting by asking me if I had any questions.

'Why did my predecessor leave?' sprang from my lips, my thoughts finding a voice, as I had been wondering why an employee would leave such a pleasant working environment with such personable colleagues. I instantly regretted my question, as it raised a look of disapproval from Patrick. He bluntly replied, 'We had a difference of opinion over responsibilities, and she was so disagreeable when Neil and I met her one day that we felt it was time she left. She had been in charge of Eden House for 16 years.'

Patrick swiftly moved the conversation on, telling me about the large donation we had received to extend Eden Hospital by 12 beds. I felt a childish excitement when he informed me that we'd go on a shopping trip soon to purchase some of the equipment. However, his upbeat mood seemed to be fading when his cold tone of command instructed me to go to Eden House to spend the day with Barbara. Conversation clearly over, I turned and left with dignity.

Mystified at the sudden dismissal, I drove to Eden House using the street map that my organised hubby had bought me. The journey seemed longer than on the previous hasty tour. The daylight did no favours to the dilapidated building, which greeted me with its dingy door, the paint peeling. I found the administration office. Voices were talking, the door ajar.

THE CATALYST NURSE

'When is this woman coming then?' a male voice asked sharply.

'What is she going to do? She is not sharing my office,' a woman responded. I could hear the indignation in her voice as I momentarily wondered who they might be talking about. Walking in hesitantly, my cloak of confidence slipped as I faced pink-haired Barbara Lewis, who I'd previously met at Church House. Slyly, she slid her arm around my shoulder, and for some reason, I thought of a snake.

'Let me introduce you to our new principal nurse, Sue,' Barbara hissed to the other occupants of the room. The hackles on my neck rose because I really did not appreciate this informality. 'Mrs Lauri' would have been much more appropriate and respectful of my position.

The insincere, over-friendly approach continued as further introductions were made. I tried to read their faces. The sister in charge, Lynda, a small woman in her mid-40s, stood by the filing cabinet, eyeing me up and down. My outstretched hand, waiting for a handshake, fell to my side as her steely gaze looked through me. I forced a smile, saying how pleased I was to meet her, before turning to Mike, a smartly dressed man leaning against the wall. The awkward atmosphere lingered as Barbara herded me out, informing me of the intensive tour she would take me on and that I could catch up with the others later.

The 'tour' commenced in the room, which had made its shabby, cobwebbed mark on my memory with its rose-pink wallpaper. The spiders appeared to have spun even more webs, and I began to feel like a fly trapped in a spider's web when Barbara hurried me through this tiny room to a door. I wondered if they should issue me with roller skates as all anybody did was rush me around! Barbara came straight to the point and told me that this inner room would be my office. My positive and cheery demeanour fell, and my head hung low with disappointment at the tiny office with its musty, uninviting smell.

My signature 'speak my mind' approach decided to display itself as I enquired when the cleaners would be available. Barbara assured me that now the room was to be repurposed, it would be given a clean. I scowled at the foul pink carpet edged with dirt, which would not offer a professional look to my office. Barbara patronised me by pointing out how lovely it would be for me to sneak in and out of my office by the French doors, ignoring my request for a professional carpet clean.

She didn't appear to notice my look of disgust, ushering me out towards the chapel, nor did she look ashamed of the grubby rooms through which we passed on our way. I stopped to gaze into a glass cabinet full of what could be described as pre-loved garments. Barbara informed me that we were in 'Petticoat Lane'. A well-worn boned corset, faded pink, stared out at us as Barbara explained these items were for sale by residents for other residents to purchase. I thought she might be joking, but her straight face told me otherwise, and I wondered who on earth would buy such a worn-out undergarment.

We continued our stroll along the darkened corridor, and Barbara's body language revealed to me that she was well aware of its failing safety standards as she held my arm to ensure I did not trip on the uneven flooring. The true colour of the paint on the half-panelled walls could no longer be determined. My nostrils flared with the overbearing stink of urine. Barbara's explanation that we were passing the men's toilets did not need to be voiced, and, throwing etiquette to the wind, I held my nose.

Barbara produced a large key as we arrived at the heavy oak doors, inviting me inside the 100-year-old Eden Chapel. Showing no respect for the hushed tones that would usually be expected in a place of worship, Barbara suddenly decided to shower me with the details and responsibilities of her own post.

'I work for Courts, it's a management advisory company. The church employs me three days a week to advise on necessary improvements to give the residents of Eden House and the church's other establishments good quality care.'

I gulped as I stared her in the face, trying to think of the politest way of letting her know I thought she seemed to be facing a huge task. However, if the poor woman was going to try her best to implement such improvements, I would be more than willing to support her.

The odiferous chapel felt unused with its curtains of cobwebs. My mind shot ahead to opportunities we could create, such as church services for the residents followed by coffee and cake, as we had done back home at my Cornish church. A burning arrow from Barbara's mouth shot down my enthusiasm. 'No way do we allow food in church.'

Embarrassed, I hid my reaction by stooping to open a nearby chest. Tears were pricking my eyelids, the culmination of the morning's disappointments compared to yesterday's highs.

Trying to regain composure, I pulled out bundles of clothing wrapped in browning greaseproof paper. Barbara told me they were the robes the vesting clergy wore, and I instantly thought how unwelcoming and disrespectful such offers of rags would be. Barbara explained the woman in charge of the clerical clothing and artefacts had, in fact, resigned with the previous matron. Further alarm bells rang as I wondered just how many staff had resigned in recent times.

Barbara excused herself, instructing me to wander around and find my bearings and to dream up plans which I could later discuss with Lynda and Mike.

Puppy.

4. THE ROLLERCOASTER OF EMOTIONS

What a difference a day makes, I ruefully thought as I found a bench in some sunlight in the hope sitting there would cheer me up. The day before, I had been in heaven; now, I could see the steps down to hell, but I was determined not to tread them. My cheese and pickle brown sandwich awoke memories of happy times on my lunch breaks back in England. My mind tormented me by asking why we had ever set sail for this new life.

I instructed myself to make a plan, determined to talk to some residents to find a way forward to increase their quality of life. I reminded myself to accept that the standards and ways of life here might be different to what I had become accustomed to in England, but I could adapt.

I lifted my head high and marched back to the office. Finding it empty, I decided to sit in the lounge in the hope of conversing with actual residents.

I smiled to myself at the thought of those corsets as I walked down Petticoat Lane. Swear words, followed by a clatter, awoke me from my musings. Pills rolled towards me along the filthy corridor. I looked into the room from where they spilt out. A nurse crawled out, picking them up, and I watched in horror as she randomly popped pills into one of the egg cups she had repositioned on her tray. On closer inspection, I saw that each egg cup held a scrap of paper with a patient's name scrawled on it. The nurse scowled as she noticed my presence, indignantly refusing my offer of help. Clearly, she did not have a clue about my position when I challenged her actions. I was left dumbfounded by her reply that none of the concerned residents knew what medication they took, so it was no problem if the wrong pills were in the wrong cup. For a second, I dared to hope this was her humour, but I realised it was the terrible truth. I knew this must be rectified immediately: it was a life-threatening situation not only due to the wrong treatment being administered to patients but also because that floor was surely alive with germs.

This was definitely an area for immediate rectification, but Lynda spotted me and called me over to where she was about to address the residents in the lounge.

'They have appointed a principal nurse,' she began, and abruptly ended my introduction after those six words – hardly a warm or informative welcome. She obviously thought her news about the new wall clock and seating arrangements, plus the purchase of a coffee table was more interesting and important. I noticed smiling faces, an indication that the residents welcomed change. Hearing that real improvements were taking place lifted my spirits.

With renewed hope, I left the room, only to pass the egg-cup-bearing nurse. A waft of wind blew the paper names out of a few of her cups, and I froze as I watched her stoop to retrieve them, pushing the papers in any cup which took her fancy. She cheekily winked at me, leaving me rooted to the spot, absolutely speechless, with the sense I had just witnessed a murderer in action.

I arrived at the main office to find a woman lingering outside who brusquely informed me that she wanted to see Lynda, the woman she had been told was in charge.

'Lynda is in a meeting at the moment. Can I help you? I am the new principal nurse,' I offered, noticing tears brimming in the woman's eyes. I invited her into the privacy of the office, where I seated us next to each other in an attempt to make things feel more relaxed. It seemed to do the trick as she said, 'You're English, aren't you? I'm Gladys, and I emigrated to New Zealand with my husband, John, from Liverpool 30 years ago.'

Noting her worn clothes and shoes, I realised this might not have been a financially successful move for them. Her worried face added to my theory that life in New Zealand had not gone smoothly for them. She poured out her life story with no prompting from me, and I felt saddened to hear that her husband suffered from multiple sclerosis, the reason he was now a resident in this home. She explained how he had lost three stone in the 18 months he had resided here. I was shocked beyond belief as she described how he was forced to take water tablets, which made him urinate frequently and resulted in dizzy spells. She rubbed her eyes as she told me about her lack of sleep due to worry. I knew from my extremely recent experience that her husband's medication was probably not always correct.

THE CATALYST NURSE

Suddenly, the door shot open, and our privacy was invaded by the angry voice of Lynda barking at me, 'Just can't wait to get into my office, can you?'

I stood up to exert my authority over the rude woman, but before I spoke, Lynda pushed her shoulders back to gain a greater stance over me, her eyes directing me to leave. 'I'm sure Lynda will be able to help you, Gladys,' I said, not quite able to conceal my sarcastic tone.

It was 4:30 p.m., so I decided to drive home and work on my plan, realising I needed to make a list of my questions plus suggestions for ideas I hoped to implement. My mind was going round in circles as I considered all the major issues which needed to be rectified. I had observed a total lack of care and nursing knowledge.

I tried to cheer myself up by stopping to buy lamb chops for tea. All my friends in England would be jealous of New Zealand lamb chops – at least one thing about our move was positive. I knew they imagined they were so nice that we'd even have them for breakfast! I pulled in at the Merry Vale shopping centre for my chops, but the butcher told me the only remaining ones were coated in breadcrumbs, apparently meant for the barbecue. They looked rather small to me. It was the straw that broke the camel's back when my husband commented the chops were not bad for my first attempt and then sat back to watch his precious sport on the television, leaving me to clear away. Life here felt like one huge anticlimax, and I had to fight, once more, the tormenting thoughts as to why we had left behind family and friends for all of today's disappointments.

THE CATALYST NURSE

I took Bobbie off to Hagley Park, and as he chased a family of ducks into the river, I relaxed sufficiently to contemplate how I should move forward to improve the awful conditions at Eden House. I told myself that apart from the unacceptable egg cup distribution of drugs and the offhand attitude of some staff, things were not a complete disaster. I just had to decide who to approach with my new ideas. I discounted the thought of Barbara and Patrick, who had both displayed a wary attitude towards me.

I reminded myself that I would need to develop a new mindset in New Zealand because everything was so much more casual. I had noticed in my maternity post that during the lunch break at the hospital, cleaners would sit with nurses, doctors and consultants. It was a very egalitarian society. In contrast, back in England, the nurse managers had their own carpeted toilets. It was also customary to address nurses and members of the public by their surname, not an abbreviation of their Christian name. I realised I would need to gain some further management skills.

The following morning, I felt brighter and appreciated the fact that Tom and I now worked the same hours. Our new life wasn't so bad after all. I turned a deaf ear to his grumpy moans that I had to do something about Bobbie's morning walk, which was not satisfactory, according to Tom, because I had kept him leashed.

The shining sun seemed to echo the more positive thoughts which filled my mind as I drove towards Christchurch. In the past, I had found driving home along Fitzgerald Avenue between 9 and 10 p.m. after a late shift at the maternity unit hazardous. Young men with Rastafarian hairstyles would jump onto the front of my car for a joyride or try to open the doors to hijack my car. Tom had instructed me, at the time, to ensure I locked all my car doors, and there had been times when I was so glad I had listened to his advice. It was frightening to have a man's full face press against the windscreen as he sprawled across the bonnet, not to mention the scratches on the car these maniacs left behind. Another advantage in Christchurch was parking – I managed to find a parking spot close to Church House most days.

All these thoughts added to my upbeat mood as I arrived at Church House at 8:50 a.m. with a much lighter step than when I had left the previous night. I almost ran up the stairs! All memories of grumpy hubby's parting words were dismissed as I wore my cheerful smile despite the threatening high humidity of the day. I decided an area to commence my actions was paramount. I wanted the team of nurses to experience every eventuality they could possibly encounter in a nursing environment. I decided a good starting point would be for me to discover how nurses and nursing assistants worked in New Zealand; I couldn't assume it would be the same as in the UK.

I was struggling with the high temperatures – my Scottish ancestry had not equipped me with genes to cope with this new climate – but today, I was going to see the climate as a positive. As I approached Patrick's door, the ultra-shining brass handle dazzled me. He was clearly a man who liked to work in an extravagant environment. Patrick, smartly dressed as before, sat behind his ordered desk, coloured files neatly displayed – an image to inspire confidence. My heart skipped as he looked up and told me that he would like to pop some dates in the diary for us to choose the furnishings for the new hospital wing. My contentment continued as I savoured this professional approach. He promised me a new desk and chair for my office. Thrilled by his obvious commitment to improvement, I plunged into explaining all my observations of things that needed rectifying. In full flow, I described all the atrocious issues I had spotted on my previous day's trip to Eden House. Like a mousetrap banging down, he immediately halted my enthusiasm.

'I don't want to be diverted from my present task, Sue. It would be best if you discussed any problems you have with Barbara, she is the one organising staff at our present homes. I am developing the new hospital wing and Butler's Park. Oh, you won't know about Butler Park – it is a new site we are developing in Christchurch close to the River Avon. Very exciting. You must talk to Barbara and the new chief nurse in charge of it; perhaps you could arrange to meet up one day with Neil and Daphne. Let me return to the task at hand. Could we make a date for next Monday to purchase the necessary items? You will need to make a list of everything we will need.'

Hope remained in my heart as we fixed the time. Patrick was looking downward, sorting his files while he spoke. 'We can visit the hospital first and then go on to some wholesale units I know of in Christchurch.' I had noticed there was very little eye contact between us.

'If there is an increase in the number of patients, we will need more nursing staff to cover the care,' I pointed out. Patrick stopped what he was doing, looked directly at me and said, with a sneer in his voice, 'Oh, well, while you are sorting out the furnishings, you can give me your thoughts on the number of nurse aids and volunteers you think we will need.'

'Surely the number and type of nurses is a statutory requirement,' I replied.

'You must remember we are a charity and have to make every dollar count. We rely on donations for our work. Yes, we have been given $40,000 for the hospital, but the church invests that money, and we can only spend the interest it gains.'

I sat quietly, the silence uncomfortable, while Patrick continued to rummage among the files. Eventually, he broke the silence. 'There is an evening meeting next Wednesday night when members of the development committee will be present. You may like to attend not only to view and to learn from the proceedings but also to meet the members of the committee.'

I made a note in my diary, fully intending to attend. I asked, 'Are there any fundraising activities taking place to help towards the cost of the patients' and residents' wellbeing?'

Patrick stared at me, a questioning expression on his face.

'I was thinking of something like afternoon teas on the lawn outside the hospital or champagne and strawberry breakfasts. I've hosted both before. They would make quite a lot of money and help people to join forces and support projects.'

Patrick sat back in his chair, looking aghast. 'Afternoon tea? Champagne breakfasts?' He smirked.

'Yes, you know, cream cheese and cucumber sandwiches, scones with strawberry jam and clotted cream, perhaps some fancy cakes or biscuits, tea or other beverages as well. We could also have raffles with wine, spirits, chocolates or other gifts – this would make the event more enjoyable and make lots of money.'

My face fell as I registered his disdain at my suggestion. My nostalgic mind wandered to the time I had held such an event back in England for the publishing company where Tom worked. Patrick was clearly a man who spoke his mind regardless of the feelings of others. He sharply reminded me that I was working for a hospital and that I had better things to concentrate on.

I stood up and left feeling totally deflated again. I felt like my emotions had been on a rollercoaster these last few days, one minute on a high, the next on a low; it was all very unsettling. Wallowing in my self-pity, I bumped into Pat.

'Hello, Sue, isn't it? I am Pat, the secretary, remember me from your interview? Would you like to have a meal with us one evening? I know life is different in New Zealand. How are you settling in?'

I felt like hugging this British woman after the cold treatment from Patrick. Thoughts of home flooded my mind, and I hoped that this was not the start of homesickness.

I returned to my car, fancying an early lunch. As I ate my sandwiches, I tried to be positive again. The weather was unbelievable: just one sunny day after another with very little wind, unlike Cornwall, where they could have four seasons in one day and always a wind or light breeze. You could never go out without a raincoat or some sort of head covering in case it rained. This was truly something to be grateful for! Reminiscing, I recalled how Tom would often take me to Charlestown, where we would sit in the car, parked at the top of the hill, to watch the sea engulfing the harbour wall with waves so high they were awesome, even at a distance the raw force of the sea could be clearly heard. On one occasion, a police car had parked on the harbour wall in a coastal town in Cornwall when mighty waves rose over the wall, engulfing the police car and taking it out to sea. Both police officers died.

 I dragged my mind back to the present and drove to Eden House. The bright sun showed up the dull grey windows, which shouted out that they had not been cleaned for many years – another thing on the list to discuss with Barbara in our next meeting. As I parked the car, I noticed the unkempt gardens. Having arrived early, I decided to explore the grounds and was delighted to discover a large field where some beautiful trees overhung a shed. I spotted three lady residents sitting in the shade of its protruding roof and seized the opportunity for a chat, commenting on their knitting. I hoped to discover their opinions on life in Eden House. I soon realised from their responses that I might not gain the information I would have liked, as sadly, they were all in the grip of dementia. I continued chatting to the lovely ladies about the beautiful butterflies and birds which were circling us. There was a disgusting stink from the open doors of the shed. Looking inside, I saw the expected garden equipment and, behind some boarding, a mound of grass cuttings, so I assumed I'd identified the cause of the stench. My heart missed a beat as I spotted two covered bundles, the shape clearly revealing corpses. On closer inspection, I realised the bodies were wrapped in bed sheets.

5. RISING ABOVE THE STORM TO FIND THE SUNLIGHT

I stood there stunned. Lynda appeared to call the residents for lunch. As the ladies wandered together towards the dining room, I grabbed Lynda to demand an answer to why there were bodies stored in the shed. I was further shocked when she explained they were from the hospital – this had been the practice for the last ten years. Bodies were always stored there until the undertaker could collect them. She informed me I'd have to see the sister in charge of the hospital if I was unhappy with the situation, but I could tell she saw nothing wrong with the present arrangement. To me, it was just another indication of how residents were mere numbers – they were shown no genuine compassion or respect, even in death.

I had an appointment with Barbara at Church House at 10 a.m., but it did not surprise me in the slightest when she failed to show. I had already assessed that she felt she gave herself some power by keeping people waiting. A tap on my shoulder indicated her arrival – another tactic, I suspected, for appearing superior by hoping to startle me. I turned to face her, finding her casually dressed in a revealing white top, her pink mop of hair doing nothing to contribute to a professional appearance.

'You haven't seen much of Hardwick Court, have you?' she said as she greeted me.

'No, Neil was going to take me after my interview, but by that time, it was getting dark, and time was short, so we didn't visit,' I replied.

'I want to introduce you to the matron; she is interviewing for staff and would welcome support and, of course, another opinion,' Barbara continued. 'Hardwick Court is the newest of the homes and is for residents who are mostly independent but need a little reassurance.'

I suddenly felt that maybe I could see past the pink hair and arrogant attitude – this was the exact type of experience I was seeking.

The house was situated in a more upmarket and expensive part of Christchurch. We approached, driving through fertile gardens with lush green manicured lawns that contained shaped multicoloured flowerbeds, creating a welcoming and relaxing atmosphere. A large, modern, one-story building containing a windowed corridor adjoined the residential section on one side, with a large reception and administration block with several meeting rooms on the other. I could not help but be impressed as we entered the building through gleaming glass doors; my mind immediately made comparisons with Eden House.

Finding Matron's office, we entered and saw Michele, a young woman of about 20, sitting behind her desk. Her haughty demeanour encompassed the room. Why was I surrounded in this new post with so many staff who thought themselves above their expected duties? I soon discovered

THE CATALYST NURSE

that Michele had been given the position of matron, having just qualified as a nurse! The fact she had been a nursing assistant before her training and knew all the residents well was apparently more important than qualifications and experience. Michele ordered a tray of tea as we waited for two applicants for a nursing assistant role to arrive for their interviews. Michele and Barbara had roped me into being on the panel, but I welcomed this opportunity.

I favoured the first applicant as she had knowledge of the nursing world, had a kindly attitude and seemed very keen to work at the home. However, I saw a red flag waving above the management of this establishment when Barbara and Michele agreed the second applicant was more suitable, explaining she could be trained in their ways of doing things. I registered how my strong, independent approach was probably a huge disappointment to my managers.

Interviews over, I was invited to meet the residents in the dayroom. They were not hidden from me, as in Eden House. The two homes could not be compared. No filthy green corridors here; the glass doors decorated with illuminated flowers were a sight to behold.

Michele and Barbara were not shy about dropping surprises on me. We entered the day room, which was equipped with a stage and microphone, and I was informed that I was the guest speaker! As a midwife and community nurse, I had given many talks to students and the general public on health issues, so I was no stranger to a microphone. Relieved that I was suitably dressed for this surprise, I addressed the lady residents. I could tell Barbara was disappointed that I had not been thrown by this little plot of hers, and to realise that it was actually working in my favour when she saw the interested look on the faces of the residents as I spoke and shared my qualifications, experience, background, aims and objectives for my new post. I explained I wanted to make their lives happier, and I was delighted that some of the residents had questions for me when I had finished my speech. The lady who asked me if I knew her brother, Brian Higgins, from Liverpool, was sadly disappointed when I did not. Another asked me if I sometimes found it difficult to find where my patients lived when I had been a district nurse, so I regaled her with a tale.

'Yes, I have sweated and worried many times trying to find where a patient lived. One time, I had just taken the position of district nursing sister and received a call at 3 a.m. to visit a pregnant lady. I asked for some instructions, as I realised she lived in a very rural area. I was told it was first left by the public house, past the cottage with the broken gate and up the lane past the cherry tree, then on my right to look for a row of cottages – theirs was the one with the new roof. I asked the caller to put on all the lights in the cottage to give me a helping hand.

'I felt like Sherlock Holmes as I tried to follow those instructions. It was winter and dark, so the cherry tree would have no leaves and look little different to any other tree. I said a little prayer for help, and then suddenly, in the distance, I saw a cottage with all the lights on, and my headlights caught the gleaming tiles of the new roof.'

THE CATALYST NURSE

The attentive ladies had come alive, and I caught a slight green tinge to Barbara's complexion – the little green monster of envy, I was sure. Their questions flowed.

'Have you ever been frightened in your job?'

'Oh yes, many times. The one occasion that sticks out in my memory the most is when I visited a dying man in another rural location in Cornwall. This gentleman needed to have a painkilling injection every four hours. It was before the time of the syringe drivers we use today. He wasn't my patient, so I knew nothing about him, only that his wife would not be there and the key to the front door would be on a hook sticking out of a post by the door. I found the house and then the key to the door; however, by the key was a straw dolly used to denote membership of the occult. At least I had a warning. Entering the house, I saw there was an empty room with a large round sheepskin rug in the middle of the floor. I moved the rug as I walked over it and saw a white circle painted on the slate floor. Calling out to anyone in the house, I made my way up a narrow staircase to a small bedroom, where I found my patient in bed. All the medical equipment and drugs he needed were on a table by the side of the bed. After introducing myself and having a short preliminary conversation, I made up the drug and administered it to him. I had been asking him about himself prior to the injection, and his response seemed relaxed and friendly. After the injection, he asked me if I would stay with him until his wife came home. She was only across the road and would return very shortly. He was my only late call that night, so I agreed and pulled up a stool by his bed, and we continued our chit-chat.

'The hairs suddenly started to rise on the back of my neck as I realised the music coming from the church across the road was not church music. I looked at my patient, and he stretched out a bony hand from under the sheet and held on tightly to my arm. His eyes were full of anxiety, and I could sense his fear. I found myself with my arms around him, saying the Lord's Prayer. We both heard the door open and footsteps on the stairs. I saw the hairs on her chin coming through the door first as a bent old lady, holding a shawl, entered the room. I shot out of the house into my car and locked all the doors. If there were bad spirits, locking the doors would not have helped me. I drove out of the village like a bat out of hell. The man died two days later.'

I had captivated my audience; one could have heard a pin drop. Barbara's face revealed her disdain that I had created such a rapport with the residents. She robbed me of any opportunity to speak to the audience individually as she opened the door, indicating I was to leave.

My head was all over the place. One moment, I loved the challenge of this new post; the next, I felt it was hopeless, that I was banging my head against a brick wall. Everywhere I turned, there seemed to be a member of staff determined to block my aims and objectives. Writing home to my parents was therapeutic because it helped me to remember the good points of our new life; there was no way I was going to reveal my disappointments to worry them. I had always felt that they had assumed my sister would have a more successful life because she had attended the grammar school. So, sitting down to write my regular letter to them, my spirits were lifted as I mentioned all the advantages of the life I knew had caused so much light-hearted envy among family and friends back home.

Dear Mum and Dad,

As always, I must tell you about the lovely sunny weather which allows us to spend more time outdoors. We love to take Bobbie to the park, and this weekend, we are going to visit Lyttleton on the coast. It is a main port for South Island. It is the gateway to Canterbury, where the first four ships of settlers landed in about 1850. Lyttleton Harbour sits in an eroded crater of a volcano, or so a girl at work told me.
I am trying to persuade Tom to take up golf with me. It is very cheap to learn and play here compared to the UK, and it would be very relaxing. Rugby is the main sport here, or should I say religion? Whenever there is a rugby match at the QE11 Park in Christchurch, the supporters are in gangs; one called the Mongrel Mob and the other the Black-hand Gang. Some staff at work take a day off to support them. No one seems to mind. Imagine if we did that in the UK, the sister in charge would blow a fuse.
Tom is going to video the last performance of the premier award-winning ice skaters Torvill and Dean tonight. It is their final performance in England and is on for an hour. We thought we would keep it for posterity.

THE CATALYST NURSE

On Monday, they are showing the Royal Variety Performance from the Palladium Theatre in London. I feel it is my patriotic duty to watch it.

Why don't you have a fluffy kitten, Mum? Cats look after themselves and don't need walkies. A kitten would keep you busy playing with it. Then, as they get older, they are nice and cuddly. I better go now as I can hear Tom's car going into the garage, and I haven't started to prepare dinner. Tom seems to like his new job.

Look forward to your letters.

Love Sue, Tom and Bobbie

Rereading my letter, I thought how perfect our new life sounded. I had only told truths, and there were omissions, but it would not have been right to include all of my niggling worries. Bobbie ran to the door in excitement as it opened, brushing himself across Tom's legs in a welcome. I wish I could have been as enthusiastic as the little dog when hubby returned, but years of his controlling behaviour, however well meant, had taken their toll. Was I too placid? I had tolerated my parents treating me as inferior to my clever sister, and I felt Tom always saw me in such a light, too. Maybe this was why I was so determined to be forthright in this new post. People seemed to want to trample me, but they had underestimated me – I would rise up each time they tried such tactics. Maybe this determination arose because the outcome would affect not only me; too many people depended on me to make a difference.

6. A MARRIAGE NOT MADE IN HEAVEN

My marriage had not been easy, but I was a person who always tried to see things from the other person's point of view and a person who could cope with challenging situations and persevere. If Tom and myself had a disagreement, Tom would not speak to me. In the early years of our marriage, he would say, 'I will not speak to you for six weeks.' After this period, communications would resume as normal. During the silent period, I would cry and beg to be forgiven. I would lay out his clothes for the following day, prepare his favourite meals and buy him presents, such as new underwear or his favourite rum truffle chocolates. In each year of our marriage, there had been between three weeks and nine months of this mental cruelty. Once I started studying for courses – something he completely resented – there was no time limit put on the period of silence. I felt Tom saw his controlling behaviour as his way of looking after me, but he always thought his way was the right one and, as you will have noticed, his actions did not feel loving at times, and as the years rolled on, I began to prefer my own company to spending time with him.

One evening, Tom walked in. 'Hope to goodness it's not lamb again,' he grunted. As always, I responded with a pleasant comment asking about his new job. He did not have a clue about how I really felt as I returned home each night. He always washed with Imperial Leather soap, believing its lingering fragrance, enhanced by the same brand of deodorant and talcum powder, added to the overall impression he gave of sophistication. The moment my nostrils identified the scent, my stomach began to churn, almost as it had when I had suffered the stench of the rotting bodies and the men's urinals. I had learnt to breathe deeply at these times to control the feelings of panic his controlling presence induced. I wanted to scream, to shout *Go away, stop it, I don't deserve this.* However, I managed to look calm as he responded to my enquiry about his day.

'OK, everyone seems friendly and so much more laid-back; the boss calls me by my Christian name. Oh, and I'm going to be away quite a lot, anything from two nights to a week. I have Wellington, Pickton, Nelson, Blenheim, Lyttleton, Akaroa and Kaikōura on my patch. You will have to look after Bobbie while I'm away. Still, he will be good company for you.'

After pouring himself a drink, Tom sat on the sofa, his long legs stretched out in front of him. He turned the television on while I finished cooking dinner. How nice it would be if Bobbie was a human and could offer the company Tom didn't.

'There are far more opportunities over here to get on, I think,' Tom continued. I took his words as a sign that maybe everything would work out well after all.

The next morning, ignited by Tom's words as a sign, I dressed in a straight dark-blue skirt and frilly cream blouse and felt very much the professional nurse manager as I left for my shopping trip with Patrick. I had prepared lists of what I thought were essential purchases.

Patrick took immediate charge. 'We will start at Aqua-clean for the cleaning and hygiene materials. They should be helpful with suggestions for improving the hygiene of the new wing.'

I wondered why we weren't buying things for the old wing, which was clearly in desperate need of improvements. We spent over an hour discussing spirit handwash, soaps, blow-dryers for hand hygiene, roller towels and paper towels, waste bins with foot pedals and some with floating lids. However, I felt Patrick rudely ignored any of my suggestions or contributions. Each item was costed, and a file of papers with costing on was handed to Patrick.

Finally, he asked me what was in use at present. I described the dirty pieces of worn towelling on a nail by each sink, but my obvious disgust had no effect, as he responded, 'I'm sure they are changed daily, so I think we will continue with the same in the new wing.'

He was not interested when I asked about cross-infection and the risk posed by such rags to the personal hygiene of both patients and nurses. His response of 'Poppycock' no longer surprised me. All my professional advice was falling on deaf ears, so I wondered why Patrick had even bothered to invite me on this trip. Insulted by his response, I regained my composure by looking through the booklets on beds and bedding. I took a deep breath to assert my opinion when Patrick asked me which beds were already in use. In very positive terms, I explained the need for more modern beds, which rose and fell with the touch of a button. One major advantage would be the cutback of nurse absences due to injured backs.

This type of bed would also ensure patients could get in and out of bed independently without falling. The specialist beds could move patients into sitting positions without them having to call for a nurse, so time would be saved. The speciality beds could also be fitted with cot sides if a patient suffered from confusion.

Success! I thought I must have misheard when Patrick agreed to buy 12 such beds. My positivity gauge was sky-high now, and it practically hit the roof when he said he was also going to buy special mattresses plus four pillows for each bed! I was over the moon; this would help to make a huge difference to the quality of care for the residents.

Furniture was item number three on the list. Once again, Patrick knew the place to buy such things at wholesale prices, the owner of the shop being a member of the church. Wing-backed easy chairs, upholstered in a washable tartan material, were purchased for the hospital day room. Bedside cabinets with a front cupboard and drawer were selected from a catalogue. We also bought a television table and a coffee table. None of these were my exact choices, but I was still overwhelmed by my victory concerning the beds. Tom's prediction was coming true!

Office furniture was next, and Patrick went ahead with his own decisions, buying a desk without drawers for me but refusing to purchase a chair, claiming we could use one we already had. As we were leaving the showroom, Patrick noticed a dark oak desk similar to the one we had already purchased but with drawers attached and a high-backed padded office chair upholstered in cream-coloured leather. He purchased these two items without any explanation, and I wondered who they could be for as his own desk was already superior. I wondered if one was for a certain pink-haired lady.

Wedding photo, 25.11.1967.

7. FROM BAD TO WORSE

We returned to Eden House for lunch and exchanged pleasantries; I enjoyed conversing with Patrick about his farming background. He seemed to relax, to lower his arrogant barrier, but suddenly, as if remembering himself, he sat bolt upright in his chair, stretched out his arms and took a deep breath as if regaining his composure. I seized the opportunity as I sensed we were to speak professionally again and came straight to the point: 'Coming back to the present day, I'm not too sure about the care at Eden House. When residents are taken ill in the night, they are taken by stretcher to the hospital. Patients die in the corridor on the stretchers while waiting for the hospital day staff.'

'Well, does it really matter where they die?' Patrick snapped. 'Do they mind?'

Stunned, I nearly fell off the old chair Pat had found for me to sit on. 'Look, Sue, these people haven't worked hard and saved their money for their old age. Why should we pamper them?'

Speechless, I left the office and made my way to the car. I felt as if he had slapped me in the face. This was becoming the daily pattern of ups followed by downs. Why was the callous Patrick working for a Christian organisation? I tried to comfort myself with the knowledge that I would appeal, the following day, to Barbara for some moral support.

I wondered what other unacceptable approaches I would encounter, and I did not have long to wait because on my next visit to Eden House, I arrived to find a police car parked outside. I ran in, concerned about what problem there might be. Lynda insulted me by letting out a groan as she saw me (at least I kept mine silent on seeing her!). However, I stopped in my tracks when I discovered the police officer enjoying a laugh with her.

Haughtily, with a wave of her hand, Lynda trivialised the information that $600 had gone missing from the safe. The police officer seemed just as unconcerned when he explained he had given her a reference number and assured me that the insurance would pay out. As he nonchalantly left, I demanded to know more details. The story was that the safe door had been found open, and the money that had gone missing was from the residents' pocket money. I wanted to know who had access to the safe.

'Look, this happens in homes where people have dementia. We will get the money returned through the insurance. There is no problem; it has happened before.' Lynda spoke quietly as if she was trying to calm me down, dismissing the situation as if I was fussing over nothing.

I walked away in disgust, but if Patrick and Lynda thought it meant I had let the matter drop, then they could not have been more wrong. I would be making a plan to rectify all these unacceptable attitudes. I decided to pop over to the hospital and went through the shortcut passageway, where I bumped into Lynda, who was carrying dirty laundry in a bucket. Astonished, I enquired why there wasn't a laundry trolley – another thing to add to my list of urgent improvements needed.

I slept very lightly that night, anxious about my meeting with Barbara the following day. I decided to wear my badges; somehow, they might support my air of authority, which I felt I might need as I raised all the issues I had in mind. My badges were my pride – Cornwall and Isles of Scilly: General Nursing, District Nursing, State Registered Nursing, Midwifery and Hospital Nursing. The four made quite a decorative display; I did have others, but these four were the important ones.

Barbara visibly groaned as she locked eyes on my badges. What was it about these people groaning and moaning all the time? I was proud of the seven years of training my badges represented. Patrick had remarked on my badges when I met him, which had given me the ideal opportunity to explain their significance.

Barbara informed me that she was going to delay our chat because she had business to attend to at Eden Hospital. Hours later, she breezed into my office, finding me sitting by the recently cleaned French windows – one job ticked off.

'Did you enjoy your shopping trip with Patrick?' Barbara surprised me with her cheerful tone.

My tone was not so bright. 'I have some urgent things to talk about, Barbara. You said I had to tell you or Patrick before I did anything, but Patrick continually refers me to you whenever I wish to discuss anything, so you and I need to talk and take action immediately.'

I plunged into my list, starting with the need for a medicine trolley and going on to explain why medicine sheets should be allocated to each patient. I insisted each patient should have a new assessment by their doctor concerning their medication. Her sarcastic reply enquired who was going to organise all this.

I had my answer ready. 'I was told that a doctor visited every Monday morning. We could work with four patients at a time, recording their medical history, taking their blood pressure, pulse, respiration rate and testing their urine. All new patients would be assessed on admission. Doing this would help the doctor to prescribe the most appropriate medicine. We would save a lot of patients from feeling confused and from experiencing side effects to drugs that are not right for them, which may result in falls.' Giving Barbara my sternest gaze, I felt I was winning the battle, and her comment of, 'Well, I suppose you have a point,' showed me I was.

'Next, I want to discuss patient deaths. When a patient dies, I feel they need as much dignity and respect as it is possible to give. I feel disgusted that bodies are being left, wrapped in sheets, in the garden shed. We need a coffin to rest them in and a safe place for them to rest until the undertaker can collect them.'

Barbara's eyes were wide open as she spat out her reply. 'They often have more than one death in a day, and it takes the undertaker three days to deliver a coffin and collect the patient.'

'Then we must negotiate with the undertaker to supply whatever we think we need; after all, if he is leaving the coffins, he will be getting the business.'

'I'll have to discuss it with Patrick,' was Barbara's reply. I felt frustrated that the pair of them always delayed an answer by saying they would have to discuss matters with the other; it was like being on a merry-go-round.

I moved on to the problem of the missing money.

'Don't start on that subject,' Barbara strongly interjected, pointing a finger in my direction. You haven't been here two minutes; you don't understand. The people who work here are caring people but very poorly paid and hard to replace once they leave. We had an awful job with recruitment. I know, on this occasion, it was the patients' pocket money, but the insurance will replace that. Patients will not be out of pocket, and the money will have helped somebody in a crisis. Will you just leave this one alone?'

Flabbergasted, I looked at my notes before continuing. 'I want to do something about the smell around here. It is obviously caused by urinary incontinence, and as I've done the management of incontinence course, I feel we could do something to help resolve this problem. I would like to have meetings with the matrons and sister in charge to advise them and ask for their help.'

'Oh, you've done a course in everything, haven't you?' Barbara wore an insolent smile. 'The matrons want to be left in charge of their own homes, so be careful what you say. I discussed your role with Lynda the other day. She feels she wants control of Eden Hospital, as promised when she took over the role.'

My mouth fell open in surprise at all these people wanting control. Wasn't my position to be in charge of all these areas?

'Neil is meeting Daphne at Butler's Court tomorrow afternoon and wondered if you would like to join them. Neil has all the plans for the new development. You would find it interesting. Daphne is Dutch – I'm sure she'll appreciate your badges.'

I scowled, wondering if this was a sarcastic or sincere comment.

Bobbie's welcoming, wagging tail greeted me again in the evening. I realised he was the highlight of this new, unsettled life where I felt controlled by people's moods. It was becoming a regular habit to have sleepless nights as I reflected on all my interactions with the various team leaders. I had felt hurt by the disrespectful reactions to my badges and by the casual way the leaders paid little attention to the issues I had raised. There were so many points I had not had the opportunity to discuss; for example, I had wanted to discuss my idea of a confidentiality form to be signed by each employee. As I lay awake, I mentally designed one – the aim to prevent gossip by untrained staff.

Neil had asked me to call for him at his family home, which was adjacent to the Butlers Court development, where I met his no-nonsense wife. The church on the grounds of Butlers Court was our first stop. Wherever there is building work, layers of dust are inevitably evident, and Butlers Court was no exception.

Neil found a fairly clean set of chairs and a table to spread out the architect's plans for the future development of Butlers Courts. I could see the pride on his face when he began to narrate the history of this glorious house, which had been rebuilt after a colonial fire in the early 20th century, becoming the home of church members for many years. It was now to be converted into a lifecare complex and retirement village offering accommodation and healthcare to property owners with endowments, which he explained would be used, in time, to pay a substantial subsidy towards the cost of rest-home care or hospital stays. He explained how activities would cater for all interests and that residents, plus cottage residents and visitors, could use the dining room. The cottages and flats would be built in the grounds.

I felt like I had crossed over from the slums to a palace as I observed the huge differences which would exist between Eden House and here – the best address in town with the river and Hagley Park just a stone's throw away.

Neil introduced Daphne into the conversation by saying she had visited the rest homes in North Island and found them too regimented. Daphne seemed to have noticed in these homes what I had seen first-hand in Eden House. Apparently, she had already told her staff of 18 carers, six of whom were registered nurses, that it was important to talk to patients, not just leave them sitting in chairs between meals and bedtime. This is exactly what was happening under their very noses in Eden House! I didn't know whether to be happy or disgusted.

THE CATALYST NURSE

Happy because this was exactly the new philosophy needed in Eden House, but fuming because nobody was listening to me when I said exactly what Daphne had been saying.

Neil continued giving more proclamations by the delectable Daphne. 'Daphne feels there should be sofas arranged facing each other across glass-topped coffee tables; she wants to use tablecloths on the dining tables. The residents of Butlers Court should be offered sherry before dinner and menus for added personal choice.'

I could have done with a sherry right then as he continued, 'People in the cottages will be able to visit the main building, where they may have afternoon tea with their friends or meals if they don't wish to cook for themselves.' Afternoon tea! I recalled Patrick's horror at my suggestion of afternoon tea. Just what had Daphne got that I hadn't got? They were clearly going to act on all of Daphne's words of wisdom. Of course, I knew the full answers to my own contemplations. Butler's Court had foundations of wealth and the potential to create more wealth. It had residents who had been judged worthy of respect based on their backgrounds, whereas the paupers in Eden House were seen as burdens. I felt it was as simple as that, and I felt more determined than ever to be a voice for the Poms of Eden House.

Neil explained that for people who required help but wished to stay in their own cottages, cleaners and nursing care would be provided. He told us that they had a member of the church who was going to help furnish and decorate the Butlers Court main building for Daphne. Although I knew my mission was to help the folk in Eden House, I could not help but feel slightly envious of Daphne – what pleasant experiences all her proposed work would involve in such beautiful and luxurious surroundings. Butler's Court sounded like paradise compared to Eden House, but I had to remember my nursing was a vocation to help others, not a ticket to a life of luxury for me. However, I did admire Daphne – a woman with spirit, a comprehensive nursing background like myself, and common sense.

The chemistry between Daphne and Neil was obvious, and I wished Barbara and Patrick had the same conversation and eye contact with me as Daphne and Neil had with each other.

After the meeting, I offered Daphne a lift home as I passed close to where she lived. This was gratefully accepted on the proviso we had a coffee at a local store first. With the same philosophy in nursing the elderly we got on like a house on fire, which I found very encouraging.

8. A POT OF GOLD AT THE END OF A RAINBOW

I knew I could make Eden House into my own version of Butler's Court with the highest standards for all the residents; maybe not with the sherry, though! I decided to make an immediate start by popping over to Eden House in the evening to meet some of the night staff.

Entering with my own key, I noted the door to the office on the right was open; the light was on, but the room was empty. As I walked down the dimly lit Petticoat Lane, I promised myself I would abolish this gruesome corridor as soon as possible. I spotted light from an open doorway and the sound of a Zimmer frame tapping the floor. I caught up with the lady using it.

'Good evening, I'm Sue, the principal nurse. I have just come to say hello to the night staff.'

'I don't think we have any night staff on here; they will be in the hospital,' the lady said with a tone of resignation. I assumed she must be suffering from dementia to say such a thing, but I carried on chatting to the talkative and pleasant lady who introduced herself as Edith and told me she was in her 80th year. I followed her as she climbed into bed, and I sat chatting on old army blankets at the end of her bed, noticing how uncomfortable her mattress was. I spotted her thin pillow and the threadbare mat on the floor. I immediately wondered how Neil could be so enthusiastic about Butler's Court when he must have known how awful the conditions were here. Well, I now knew why he had rushed me through here so fast on my introductory pre-interview talk and why he had said the staff would not want to be disturbed – there were no staff. Edith was not demented; Neil was demented to think that this state of affairs was acceptable.

I went with Edith to the bathrooms, where I was shocked to see the child-sized facilities with a solitary handbasin for the 11 ladies on the unit to share. On leaving the bathroom, I spotted another light coming from under a door on the opposite side of the corridor. After giving a gentle knock on the door and getting no reply, I tried the handle and found it locked. I knocked once more, a little harder this time, and spoke into the side of the door. 'Hi, I'm Sue, the principal nurse, I have come to say hello.' I'd finally accepted in New Zealand I was to be called by my first name.

I heard movement inside the room, a chair sliding over an uncarpeted floor. A key could be heard turning slowly as the door slightly opened. A young girl in a nurse aid uniform stood looking out, wide-eyed, cautious, fear etched all over her face. Her fingers tightly gripped the side of the door, holding it just wide enough for her to see through.

'Can I come in and say hello? I'm the new principal nurse,' I repeated. The door was slowly opened wider, enough for me to enter. I felt I had to be very gentle with this girl who was obviously scared stiff.

Inside, the walls of the square room had fitted shelves storing dried and tinned foodstuff. I had heard rumours of food being taken home by staff. I could vaguely see a square wooden table bearing an open magazine.

'We sometimes have prowlers in and I don't like being on my own,' she said in a shaky voice.

'What do you do if someone wants you or falls out of bed?' I asked.

The girl shrugged and said, 'I wait for the day staff.'

I was at the stage where I was no longer shocked by whatever conditions I found in this place. It felt awful leaving that night realising I could not make instant changes, but I vowed to raise standards as soon as possible – although it would need something of a miracle to get this place to the standard Daphne's nirvana was going to be.

I decided to move on to the hospital where, thankfully, there was a different atmosphere altogether. Two well-built middle-aged women with open faces and kind dispositions were busy folding towels and sheets, placing them in neat rows in a linen storage cupboard on the main corridor.

They took me to the nurses office, where they told me they had worked together in Eden Hospital on night duty for over five years. Sitting in soft, comfortable chairs, they talked about the patients, the patients' relatives and their own families. A remark was made by one of the women about the new sister in charge and how she had known Neil from her school days. For some unknown reason this rang a bell in my head. It did seem that associations resulted in promotions.

We were in desperate need of new staff uniforms and I also felt they would help to boost the nurses' morale. I marched into Eden House, thrilled with my selection of various colour samples. Staff training was another subject for my research because I had noticed there was a great need for nursing development, and I planned to contact the local colleges. I wanted to apply for a management course to further my personal development. I decided to hop over to update Patrick on my latest proposals. My knock went unanswered but as I stood at the door, the administrator's words from my first day floated into my mind: 'If you want to look through the staff files, you'll find them in the top drawer of my filing cabinet.' Having been given the OK, in rather a secretive way, I sneaked into the office. The way the cabinet was organised was pleasing, as all the staff names greeted me in alphabetical order as I hesitantly pulled open the drawer. My eyes opened in amazement as I read through the files.

Lynda, who Neil had employed for her apparent ability in management and care of the aged, had previously been employed by Christchurch Hospital as an occupational therapist aid, talented in basketwork. In her distant past she had worked as a staff nurse. As if scales had been removed from my eyes, I realised her confidence had been a disguise for the fact she didn't really know what she was talking about. Barbara had suggested Lynda should refer to me if she had any questions on nursing matters. No wonder Lynda had declined, saying she wanted to pick the person to answer her queries herself – she had realised I would soon have grasped how little she understood. I opened the file of Pat, matron of Eden House. Her experience included gaining a hairdressing diploma, being supervisor of the cleaners at Christchurch Hospital, and some management instruction experience. I read that Michele had been a nurse aid at Hardwick Court prior to undertaking general nurse training. She had recently passed her general nursing certificate. She hardly had sufficient experience to be sister in charge.

Lunch break was over according to the laughter I heard drifting up the stairs, so I chose to leave this task, for now, to return to Eden House. I was pleased to find my new desk welcoming me, although looking rather ashamed of its accompanying hard, shabby dining chair. Deciding to get straight to work, I popped out for some paper from the office, passing three residents sat waiting to see the doctor. Fabulous! I assumed Pat had put into action my suggestion that patients should be assessed. Awestruck, I had stopped in my tracks, so when the doctor stepped out he wanted to know who I was, introducing himself as Doctor Black. Answering his enquiry, I decided to explain in full: 'My name is Sue Lauri, I was a district nursing sister and midwife in the UK. I am registered as a comprehensive nurse in New Zealand. I have been appointed by the church to be principal nurse. One of my objectives is to have all the residents and patients reassessed by a practising medical doctor. Correct medicine sheets filled out with a recorded medical diagnosis, where possible please. I am requesting this for both residents and patients.'

As I took a breath, he explained he had worked in Oxford and was aware of the British standards of healthcare. I took from this that he was inferring that such standards were not commonplace here.

Well, at least I had put him in the picture about what I expected. I was on a high again, and the icing on the cake was discovering that the new hospital beds had arrived and were already being made up with white bed linen and blue blankets – I felt like I had hit the jackpot! The cherry on the top of that iced cake would have been four pillows, as I had requested, rather than the two per bed I registered. Lack of nursing experience meant that Patrick had not appreciated the need for the extra two in case, for example, a patient needed their feet raised. If a patient suffered a stroke, they might have needed an extra pillow to support a limb. Sickness might result in one of the pillows needing to be laundered. However, I was impressed by the smart bed tables.

The overall result, despite the fact I could see no evidence of the extra bedpans and urinal, was a massive improvement. In reality, although it felt like I had been in this job for ages, today was showing me that I had actually achieved great things in what were really early days of my post.

As I passed the day room door, I saw Daphne sitting in one of the new high-back chairs that were covered in tartan upholstery. She looked very attractive in a green coat dress with a flowered collar. She was the sort of person who brightened one's day. Her enthusiastic comments about the chairs added to my optimism that all was to be well after such a turbulent start. She pointed out how the matching blinds added to the ambience of cosiness, and I felt proud of all I had achieved for our patients, also spotting the television table and magazine rack. Patrick arrived to tinker with the blinds, and Daphne, who was becoming a friend, left with me. I smiled as we shared a little moan about how tight Patrick was with the budget. I complained that he could not expect nurses to give good care with no equipment. Daphne had a mischievous twinkle in her eye when she informed me that he must be struggling with the budget as Neil had arranged for 40 clergy to attend a paid-for retreat at Franz Joseph, and Neil had invited her!

I decided to erase this snippet of information from my mind because I wanted to celebrate today's pot of gold, which I had found at the end of my rainbow.

Snowy mountains, from a trip I went on.

9. LIFE OUTSIDE WORK

Feeling rejuvenated, I decided to call in at the gym on the way home. After a workout, I fancied a sauna. The air was so thick I couldn't see as I entered the room. Heavy breathing and gasping alerted me to the presence of a couple doing more than having a sauna! I was not sure of the sex of either or if both were the same sex. The last few weeks had toughened me up; nothing in life surprised me now and I'd got quite good at walking out of situations which didn't impress me, so I just got up and left them to it.

As I reported it all back to Tom, he filled me in on his day and his visit to the harbour.

'You know the adverts in the local paper, about ships coming in with contents from the home country? Well, I saw a queue of people, about a mile long, coming from the harbour office today. I asked my client what the queuing was all for. It appears they were people wanting to buy goods such as Walkers crisps, Cadbury chocolate, digestive biscuits, Kit Kats, shortcake, Marmite and a whole host of products we produce in the UK but only have a limited supply of in New Zealand.'

It was good to hear about life outside my world of work. I sometimes felt that in a short period of time I was becoming institutionalised, focussed on nothing but making improvements for the residents who I didn't even know very well as my time was taken up with the constant battle to right wrongs as quickly as possible.

'Have you noticed the number of planes going over all the time, Tom?' I asked, changing the subject.

'Yes, they are practising for the Queen's visit later this month,' Tom replied as he bent over to put Bobbie's lead on. He'd offered to take him for a walk while I cooked the evening meal. Being an ardent royalist, anything to do with the monarchy was of interest to me.

'When are they coming, Tom?'

'I don't know but Mark Phillips, Princess Anne's husband, is in town, ask him.' Tom was not a royalist and his touch of sarcasm spoilt my joy.

When he returned for dinner, I tried to share the happiness I'd experienced during the day. 'What a lovely day I've had. It all started at Church House having my photograph taken for the church magazine.'

I tried, on several evenings, to share my experiences with Tom. He was not a man of many words but, if nothing else, just running through the day's activities helped to clear my mind, to refocus and see clearly for the next step forward.

'Barbara drove Lynda, Pat and I the 123 km to a geriatric hospital in Timaru. Barbara told us it was a major agricultural town for the South Canterbury region. It has a major cargo port for South Island. It's the largest populated area after Christchurch. I looked up the meaning of Timaru – it is from the Māori, meaning shelter, it meaning cabbage and Maru meaning shelter or shade.

THE CATALYST NURSE

'The nurse in charge there gave an excellent lecture on elderly care. She was one of the most enlightened people I have heard for a long time. Nursing staff at the hospital even allow animals in the ward at visiting time. She had a great depth of understanding about end-of-life care. The speaker was so animated, had such a great personality. After we had been sitting down for an hour, she made us stand up and move around to refresh ourselves.

'This lady has travelled an awful lot and told us about the Japanese lifestyle, using pictures to endorse her words. After the lecture, Barbara treated us all to lunch and we had a short time to look around the shops. The stores are so spacious, there is no overcrowding, so it is a pleasure to browse the counters in the different departments. They don't carry the stock we do at home, but then they don't have the population to create the same demand.

'Barbara was telling me her father came from the UK. He was blind and learnt how to be a chicken farmer at a college in Nottingham. It really is a small world. Barbara did say to me that she felt I may become frustrated with this job as I was an excellent nurse. I thought that was an odd thing to say, especially with all the challenges there are, what do you think?

'Barbara also invited me to play golf with her at the end of the week. I feel as if I am moving up in society. The game is on Friday afternoon but as I am giving my first report to the council on Friday evening, it's OK to have the time off in the afternoon. While listening to this lady today, I realised I am right in pushing ahead with staff education. Lynda, the sister in charge at the hospital, is doing a refresher course at Christchurch Hospital and a course on gerontology taking up one day a week. Although I can't take the credit for that, as Neil arranged it, I think he knew her prior to her appointment. Some of the nurse aids are doing study days. Do you think a management course would be helpful to me?

'Daphne and I are going to visit two elderly care homes later this week; they are run by different religious groups in Christchurch. I feel it will give us a broader perspective on what is available for the elderly, and it will also help Daphne with the development of Butler's Court.'

Looking back, did I give Tom time to respond as I emptied my mind each evening? Were my questions rhetorical or did I genuinely value his advice? He had controlled me for so long, was this my way of controlling him – making him think I needed his help when in fact I now knew my own mind and what I would do?

Yes, my life was now on a steady roll, and life in New Zealand was good. I felt respected. I had ambition, and my aims and objectives to help the residents were being fulfilled. I felt my evenings were pleasant and our future here looked good.

I had my independence at work, and I was so busy that had I turned a blind eye to Tom's controlling ways? It came as a shock when he announced the major decision he had taken without even consulting me. Tom had settled into his new job and I felt my evenings were pleasant and our future here looked good for us, and this became even more obvious when he told me his news as I arrived home.

'We had a phone call this evening from Wendy, the girl who gave us Bobbie. She wants us to have another of her Westies – seven-year-old Anna, who has lived in a kennel all her life and is no good for breeding. I told her we would love to have her but we would need a bigger house as this one has no garden.'

That was Tom for you – making all the decisions without consulting me, deciding what would be good for me. However, it felt good to have a distraction from the world of work. I didn't even try to question his decision – I had enough confrontations to deal with at work.

'I'm off to Wellington for four days, so you can keep yourself busy, don't forget Bobbie's walks, will you?' Tom was so busy with his own thoughts I wondered if he had missed most of my conversation. He continued, 'I also saw a really nice house with a double garage, a good-sized garden and a swimming pool, and we can afford it. Yes, we are going upmarket, something to tell your mum. I have arranged a visit to show you at the weekend. Do you feel your job is secure, as we will need a bigger mortgage for this house? It will be worth every dollar. We can then have the other dog, which will be company for Bobbie while we are at work; they will have a garden to play in.'

He always played the card of telling my mum when he wanted to win me over. Yes, I definitely felt that my job was secure so maybe I would join in the house viewing, why should we not better our quality of life, life was not all about work!

My mum.

10. THE KEY OF ADAPTABILITY

Things were going smoothly. Looking back, it had been a huge change moving from the UK to New Zealand and adapting to a completely new culture, but I had been prepared to accept that I needed to be more open to different ways of doing things, to the more relaxed approach. I felt the teething problems had been overcome, that people were more accepting of me and my British ways.

Relationships at work had taken a more friendly turn so I decided to ask Neil and Barbara how they thought I was performing. I needed to know that I was in a safe enough position to go ahead with the mortgage finance for the new house. I was ecstatic to hear that everyone agreed how pleased they were with my progress and liked the way I was handling matters. What a difference a few weeks had made. I felt flattered when Neil expressed concern that I was working too hard.

My admiration of Daphne had grown; in some ways, we were quite similar as we both dressed in the same professional fashion and had the same views concerning the care of the elderly. I guessed it was partly because we were both mature, comprehensively trained nurses with considerable experience. Daphne was confidence personified, but I reminded myself that I had all the necessary qualifications and my devotion and determination would uphold me.

THE CATALYST NURSE

Daphne had worked as a nurse on a passage liner, which is where she met her husband.

Together the matrons of the other elderly care homes showed Daphne and I around, and tea and cake were offered to us on both visits in brightly lit dining rooms. It was a good opportunity to exchange views and ideas. The facilities in these homes greatly outshone those of Eden House or Eden Hospital and the other two homes; they were worlds apart. The accommodation was of a higher standard, the rooms were immaculate without leaving the smell of disinfectant. There were comprehensive entertainment programmes in both premises, which catered for many interests and included film nights with evening suppers, quiz afternoons, talks by local speakers, art and craft sessions and music evenings. Each home had a large, comfortable community room and a library. Day trips were organised to places of interest. The gardens were an attractive place for residents to walk and spend time in. The relatives and friends of the residents were encouraged to visit and take afternoon tea. When asked about financial and voluntary support, the sisters in both homes were quick to say how lucky they were to have such interested members of their support committees.

Daphne's comments were favourable; like me she was in awe of the work that had been put into every aspect of these care homes. I knew Daphne hoped she could include such events and standards in Butlers Court when it was operational. I knew I would have to dream extra hard if such changes were to ever come for my Poms in Eden House.

THE CATALYST NURSE

There are so many good street cafés in Christchurch. Daphne recommended a local one she used a lot and I was willing to try it out. While lunching together, I was interested to learn more of Daphne's working relationship with Neil. She shared that she felt the tall, gentle, caring persona depicted on Neil's photograph in the church magazine, hands together in prayer, wasn't quite reflective of the man he really was. She hinted that Neil's attentions were too familiar at times. Neil had invited her for lunch at his home and when, halfway through the main course, Neil's wife approached the drive in her grey Morris Minor, Neil suddenly pushed Daphne out through the back door of the house and lifted her over the fence. Daphne landed on her hands and knees with her skirt way above her grazed knees and her tights torn to shreds. Seconds later Neil threw her handbag on the ground by her side. Naturally, the experience had made her feel humiliated and disappointed in Neil, who had never referred to it since.

Daphne was opening her heart to me and it gave me much support to realise it was not only me who saw the hypocrisy of the church. She told me how 'caring' Neil had disposed of his unwanted kittens by drowning them in a suitcase. She had received strict words from him about watching the budget for Butler's Court, yet he had spent $20 a roll on wallpaper for his office.

I filled her in on some of Patrick's shortcomings. I explained that he did not appear to like female nurse managers, not understanding their role. However, he clearly had a soft spot for Lynda, the petite, feminine sister in charge who had a subservient attitude.

THE CATALYST NURSE

Daphne listened open-mouthed as I told her about the meeting I had participated in with Patrick and Pat, discussing hygiene and incontinence, and how Lynda had disagreed with all my suggestions for improvement, which I had made based on my learning from the course I had studied: The Promotion of Continence and Management of Incontinence. I told her how the meeting had come to an unsatisfactory close, with Patrick telling me what a nice person Lynda was and how he loved her shoes! Daphne's jaw dropped further when I mentioned that Lynda was given the job because she had impressed Neil with her management skills, while Pat was a basketwork teaching assistant at Christchurch Hospital.

Daphne and I hugged each other as we said our goodbyes and that hug lasted in my heart, reminding me that I had found a soulmate who felt as vulnerable as I did in her new role. I knew we would be a support to each other as we had both seen through the charades.

11. REPORTING BACK ON THE WAY FORWARD

The committee's report was due to be presented on Friday evening; it was my first report so I was keen to make a good impression. My diary contained golf with Barbara on the Friday afternoon, which I hoped might present an opportunity to break down barriers. Organised, as ever, I decided to ensure my report was polished by Thursday evening. Tom was in Wellington for the week so I appreciated the opportunity to escape any of his input.

My conundrum was how to be honest and forthright, inspirational and motivating at the same time as being mindful not to upset my temperamental colleagues, not to come across as judgemental. Unaware of the backgrounds of the board representatives, I realised that I needed to be wary of causing any unintentional offence.

The start of the week saw us with a staff shortage in the hospital. Pious Lynda was away on a refresher course, so I thought *All hands on deck* as I donned my white uniform and offered my services. The deputy sister, Jill, was very approachable and arranged that I worked with a nursing assistant at one end of the ward while Jill worked with the other assistant at the other end.

I discovered that all the patients were to be toileted on the commode after breakfast. It was like a conveyor belt as each patient in turn had their undergarments lowered to knee level before being placed on the commode in the middle of the ward. They had learnt to hide their blushes as they sat in full view of the other beds; I could not understand why they had not, at least, been offered the privacy of a screen or the dignity of a wipe or wash afterwards. The fact that the commode was not emptied between patients was totally unacceptable.

Immediate change was needed. The assistant informed me there was no back trolley containing the necessary equipment, so I collected a bowl of water to wash the gentleman I had just attended. His faecal matter had dried so hard that when I gently wiped it, the skin was torn away. I discovered a urinal between the legs of the next patient. The slide sheets placed between legs to soak up urine offered no dignity.

In the shower room I discovered a naked female octogenarian, a stroke victim in a wheelchair — yes, this is what these Poms had been reduced to with the lack of dignity afforded them: nameless. The poor embarrassed lady tried to cover her breasts with her one mobile arm. The perforated water pipes had soaked the curtainless cubicle. She tearfully explained she had been left by the staff. I grabbed a hand towel, the only item available to offer her some modesty and warmth, as a nursing assistant appeared to wheel her back to the ward.

I recognised the symptoms of a urinary tract infection in another female patient. The ward had no urine testing kits, and I discovered that she had been prescribed sedatives, whereas antibiotics would have resolved the condition. There was no doctor to be found when I telephoned Pat, who took the opportunity to tell me that Doctor Black, who I had spoken to previously, had now left. Therefore, the patient assessment plan I had initiated would have to be put on hold until a replacement doctor could be found. I felt sick with frustration, as I had also introduced the requirement that chaperones accompany patients on doctor's appointments to ensure that a correct historical picture of the patients' conditions, treatments and medication could be presented.

It had been a rush to leave the hospital, change and arrive at the golf course looking relaxed; the two places were worlds apart. Barbara, smiling broadly, was waiting for me. She used the opportunity to quiz me on my report, which she seemed surprised to hear was complete. I guess my organised approach led to her comment that she worried I might find it frustrating working for the church. Achieving a satisfactory placing for our team as 16th, I made my apologies and slipped off home to prepare myself further for the forthcoming presentation of my report.

Presentation time felt like execution time as my sweating palm carried my briefcase with its large typed report. I had tried to think of every eventuality, as a good nurse should, and I was not going to risk being unable to read my report due to the short twilight should the interior lights be switched off. The agenda, Patrick showed me, had me placed halfway through the meeting in the main conference room.

I had gone for the style of truth and nothing but the truth. After all, my State Registered Nurse training at Treliske

THE CATALYST NURSE

Hospital, Truro, Cornwall, had taught me that nurses must always stand by their principles. Honesty was always the best policy. Nurses should act with decorum and alacrity.

The words 'Now it is over to our new principal nurse for her first report,' woke me from my thoughts. Straightening my skirt, clearing my voice, taking a deep breath, I commenced.

'Mr Chairman and members of the board.

'Over the past few weeks, I have been assessing the homes and hospital. I found the three matrons and charge nurse are keen and enthusiastic people; however, their task is an enormous one. My office is at Eden House. It is the house and hospital which are my main concerns at present.

'I observe the residents in the house, and they show boredom and confusion. Is there any wonder when you look at the appalling state of their home? The building is shabby, decaying and fourth-rate. It is a scene from a Dickens novel. The residents do have some activities but more are needed to help prevent dementia. In the hospital, I see the frozen awareness of the patients, many frail through lack of good patient care.'

I tried to close my ears to any gasps, and although I followed the good practice of looking at my audience from time to time, I tried not to read any expressions on the sea of faces. I continued, providing examples of unacceptable practice from the sisters' rosters. I referred to low staff morale, to night patients left to die on hospital corridors. There was reference to the visit by the health department, whose inspector destroyed drugs which were eight years past their expiration date. He had also logged the illegal recording of drugs. I shared my new procedures for drug administration, medical records and equipment, including medicine trolleys and sterilising equipment. I explained that I would introduce a six-monthly staff assessment plus a bill of patients' rights to enable residents and relatives to be aware of their rights and entitlements.

I shared my plans for staff training, which included Lynda and Michele attending the Nursing into the Nineties Course at Christchurch Polytechnic and myself attending a management course. Mrs Flame had agreed to provide a programme for the nursing aids. I explained costs could partly be met by new initiatives, including the selling of surplus food, which was, at present, donated.

I paused for a few seconds for effect to add meaning and strength to my closing statement.

'Mr Chairman, members of the board, at this moment our care in these areas is substandard.'

I sat to a palpable silence. A few seconds later the chairman's straight face, looking decidedly grey, stared around the boardroom table, clearly trying to assess the reaction of the board members.

He bought himself time by saying, 'Well, there is nothing like jumping in with both feet, shall we move on to the next item on the agenda?' I soon worked out that the chairman had total control of his yes-men – the board members.

The meeting concluded at 9:30 a.m. and Patrick led me out.

'These patients, residents...' *Puff.* He blew air at me. 'They are nothing to do with us, they are Brits, ten-pound Poms.

These people haven't financially contributed to our society, they have no money. We offer them shelter; they should be grateful for what they get.'

I had been prepared for his negativity but not such cruel comments. I barked back, 'All residents and patients should receive a good level of care no matter what race, colour or creed they are.' I hoped to shame him.

Patrick pushed past me, his back to me. He closed his door to me, leaving me to set off home with a barrel of emotions.

12. THE FALL

Heading for my car, I found a dark night to match my dark thoughts about Patrick's attitude. I walked quickly in the limited light. The next minute I was flat on my face with my arms outstretched, my briefcase sliding across the pavement in front of me. All the air was punched out of my body.

Tom was home. 'What the hell happened to you, Sue? You look awful.'

Tom's gaslighting style of questioning succeeded in making me paranoid – was there a possibility that I had been pushed? He had plenty to say about my report back on the meeting.

The weekend started with blue skies and sunshine – the sun always seemed to shine in Christchurch and I trusted its delightful rays to lift my mood. I tried to put work matters behind me, tidying the house while Tom took Bobbie out. Looking at the positive side of life, the purchase of the new house was going well and there was a keen buyer for our present home.

It was always therapeutic to do a deep clean of the house, but my back was hurting as I hoovered. I searched in the freezer for some ice to make an ice pack for the increasing pain.

My back was worse when I awoke on Monday morning so I arranged a doctor's appointment, informing Church House I would not be at work. Not surprisingly, Patrick sounded unsympathetic.

The doctor diagnosed a rupture of the left side of my transverse perineal muscles on the left side of my transverse Perini of one of the spinal vertebrae in the lumbar section of my spine and recommended physiotherapy. As we had only resided in New Zealand for two years, we had not paid enough money into the system so I had to pay for the treatment. I thought of all the patients I had attended in England who had only just come to live there and how we had never thought twice about their NHS treatment.

'I'm taking you out for a meal tonight,' Tom announced. 'You have had a horrendous week and we don't go out a lot. I'm told you have to take your own wine to restaurants here, so if we go to that place on Fitzgerald Avenue, we can call in at the wine and spirit store just up the road from there.'

Tom could be quite sweet at times, but I often found out he had a manipulative reason for his apparent thoughtfulness. However, today it appeared that he wanted to give me a treat to cheer me up.

Tom confessed to everyone that he wasn't the best person to pick wines – spirits were more his forte – so I popped into the warehouse-type store. Finding a suitable bottle of Chardonnay, I looked for the shortest queue at the 25 checkouts! The tough-looking cashier threw me a look of disgust before opening his mouth and booming, 'You're a bloody Pom, aren't you? You're supposed to buy cases of wine or spirits, you mean bugger.'

I wished Tom hadn't suggested getting wine.

'Take no notice of the old devil. He is just trying to wind you up,' a familiar voice came from behind. I was so glad to see a familiar face – Neil's personal assistant, Pat.

I appreciated her warmth. 'I think he fancies you really, you look so different in your evening clothes, very attractive,' she whispered in my ear as I excused myself, explaining that we had a table booked at the Chinese.

I felt hesitant about my morning return to work. Despite my cheerful greeting to Patrick, he offered no enquiry as to whether I was feeling better, despite my obvious limp and grazed legs. He asked me to drive over to Hardwick House as Michele had a problem so hadn't turned up. What a pleasant environment to work in with its luxurious atmosphere. The patients here would not be able to even imagine what the conditions were like in Eden House. I was asked to hand out the post and serve the morning coffee, which I found a pleasant task.

I had been deceived by the surface opulence. On passing a single room, I spotted the female occupant sat on a commode, trying to ring the call bell. Dashing to her aid I found her purple-faced, gasping for air. On enquiry, I discovered several of the call bells were faulty. I needed to raise this important issue with Michele, but I was informed that she was late because of an accident she had been involved with when driving the minibus, full of residents, the previous day. The patients hadn't been strapped into their seat belts, so there had been several injuries requiring hospital treatment.

Michele turned up in the afternoon and when I asked her to complete an accident form, she irritably informed me there was no such thing. She did not take kindly, either, to my suggestion that she call a mechanic to fix the call bells and, surprise surprise, she told me to see Patrick about the matter. I was, by now, so accustomed to the endless instructions to 'Tell Patrick' and 'Tell Barbara' and nothing actually getting done.

On my return home, Tom was awaiting the gossip from my day. He had arrived home early due to road blockages caused by the royal visit of Charles and Diana. I would have loved to have seen them, unlike Tom, who was not a fan of the monarchy.

After the refreshment of dinner, I felt more able to share the lowlights of my day; I'm afraid there were no highlights. The residents who were the ten-pound Poms were treated with so little respect. Tom and I were both enraged that these people, who had paid £10 to travel by sea to Australia and New Zealand many years ago when those governments were trying to increase the population and skilled workforce, were now seen as burdens to society. It was especially close to my heart because my own father had wanted to emigrate to New Zealand. They were all packed up, ready to sail, when my mother learnt that people had to live in huts until they found a house. Mum backed out, telling Dad she didn't think it was a suitable place for her two daughters, aged two and eight, to live. Dad was really upset as he had sailed to New Zealand many times when he was in the merchant navy and had made many friends here.

The next few workdays involved me covering for sick staff; nobody had shown any concern for my recent fall, but compassion was not a quality found in my place of work. I became aware of just how much food waste there was in Eden House because the menus contained inappropriate foods for the patients' requirements. The list of essential changes was now several pages long!

13. DECISIONS WHICH SHAPE DESTINY

There was the need to assess patients wishing to stay in the new hospital wing. Lynda declined my offer of accompanying me to the assessments, which I found disappointing as I had imagined it would have enhanced our relationship to work together on this task.

I realised that not all patients would be suitable and that the ones who would benefit the most would have reasonable cognitive function and some level of mobility. Patrick had made it clear that a place should be allocated for a retired vicar he knew of, presently a patient in Christchurch Hospital. His reasoning was that the placement would result in eventual financial bonus for us as the man wished to die in a church residence! On visiting the gentleman, I discovered a very sick patient receiving treatment via an intravenous infusion. The new wing would not be able to offer the level of care he needed. Patrick was fuming when he heard I had rejected this patient who clearly would have come to us accompanied by a pot of gold.

I returned to Eden House and one of the aids told me of a female resident staying in a single room who had not received a visit from staff for some days. When a member of staff did visit, she found the lady to be very frail with a mouth so dry she could not talk or eat. She was transferred to hospital on a trolley as she could no longer walk. It was just one unbelievable, diabolical discovery after another.

On the home front, I was thrilled to learn of a moving date and, of course, the swimming pool was a strong pull. I couldn't wait to write to my mum and tell her, but the next report for the subcommittee was due, so I set about completing it instead of composing the letter. I felt I should approach the report from a more positive angle because I believed, despite all the horrendous failings I kept coming across, much progress had been achieved over the past five months, which I felt would interest the committee.

I commenced boldly, saying I believed a revolution was taking place. We had made great advances in several areas. I named our two new members of staff – Daphne Madley and Mr Wade.

On the administration front, the matrons, the sister in charge and myself were producing a system which would lead to greater efficiency and understanding of the needs of the patients, improving safety for all.

Our new policies included correct procedures for recording drugs and administration. The policy of ensuring patients' medication was assessed by a doctor had resulted in several patients needing three or four less medications. Positive results had meant patients were more alert, more mobile and suffering less from the side effects of unnecessary medication.

We had now seen the benefits of the accident reports we had introduced. Assessment and dependency-rating forms had provided a medical, nursing and social history for each resident, which had enabled staff to see the patient as a whole person, not just a frail body with a dementia label. Staff assessment forms, completed six-monthly, had seen higher standards of care. Temperature, pulse, blood pressure charts, observation charts and medication sheets had also been created, with obvious benefits.

I talked about education. 'Nursing staff have been attending lectures and courses according to their rank and requirements. Lynda and Michele are attending the Into the Nineties course. Lynda is also spending three days a week at the Christchurch Hospital assessment unit as part of a reorientation programme. Pat and two nurse aids are attending the Residential Care for the Elderly course. Several nurse aids are attending the private hospitals' nursing aids course. I continue with my management course.'

This time I dared to look up at the board during my speech, as I felt proud of all the positives I was showering on them.

I went on to describe the visits we had made during the past three months to other care homes to inspire us. Daphne and I had visited many homes collecting ideas and we had further planned for Daphne to visit the church communities in Auckland in the next few months.

I moved on to speaking about the new hospital wing, celebrating the fact that it was now fully furnished and ready for occupation and that we were just waiting for health department approval. I shared how I had visited patients for the new wing to assess their suitability according to their needs, not their places in the queue.

THE CATALYST NURSE

I ventured into the area of standards in assessing patients. I explained how I planned to assess residents of Eden House and the other homes as I had come to realise many of them were intermediate or hospital cases. Talking about Eden House, I mentioned the moves in progress to deinstitutionalise residents. An activity programme had been introduced, and a budgerigar and kitten had already brought so much joy to the residents.

I shared my observations that residents from the house appeared increasingly more alert, walked with improved posture and seemed less depressed after only a few weeks. I ensured I gave due praise to the staff who were cooperating.

I spoke more about Eden Hospital, where great progress was being made to improve the quality of life for our patients.

As I read my report out, I felt proud of all I had achieved for the residents in such a short space of time. I breathed a huge sigh of relief when I had presented it, feeling that it had gone down so much better this time.

A few days later, Patrick let me know during our daily catch-up that we had an afternoon meeting with Neil and Barbara; I waited for him to explain the purpose but I looked away, embarrassed, when I realised he did not want me to know. I had such a busy day that I gave little thought to his secretive behaviour and I was shocked to find the time approaching 2 p.m. Never one to be late, I dashed across to the conference room.

The sunlit room with its lack of blinds did not help to soothe my reddened face when I arrived. Always the professional, I reached into my briefcase for my notepad but was halted in my actions by Patrick's stern voice stating that no notes were to be taken.

The dreamhouse in Hallswell, Christchurch.

14. SHOCKING SCHEMES

Neil commenced the meeting by asking me how I felt I was progressing. I was surprised at what seemed like a silly question – had I not recently shared with them all my progress in my report? Referencing that report, I highlighted again all the achievements and answered that I thought things were going very well.

Patrick spoke next and surprised me by saying Barbara had been disappointed neither to have been informed of the visits made by Daphne and myself to the other homes nor to have received feedback.

Barbara then interjected by saying she felt they needed to look at my job description. I stood my ground, reminding everyone that the subcommittee report I had written contained all the necessary information. Agitated, Patrick announced that in future, he wished to see all reports before presentation.

Neil gave me a gentle look and, speaking in a quiet manner, told me I should work alongside Patrick and Barbara, including them in all things. He added that this was not a warning and I noticed Barbara and Patrick nodding to that statement. Glancing at his watch, he declared he had to leave and the meeting came to an abrupt end.

Barbara hung back to have a quiet word with me, claiming she thought I was an excellent nurse but Neil and Patrick

THE CATALYST NURSE

simply did not know what they wanted. Speechless, I indicated my goodnight with the wave of my hand.

I was flabbergasted at the inconsistencies. My honest report was not lacking in evidence to support all the glowing progress we had made. I had received confirmation that my job was secure, that they were pleased with me. Had I just heard Barbara correctly – that she thought I was an excellent nurse? Well, she did not act like she believed that! None of these positive points had been recognised in the uncomfortable meeting I had been summoned to. I was confused.

The following few days seemed to merge into one. I had to constantly defend myself against comments thrown at me at inappropriate moments. I tried to find Patrick to discuss personnel matters, as I needed clarification on staffing issues. He wasn't available but I bumped into Neil and we both exchanged wary smiles. I was surprised when he asked about my reaction to the previous day's meeting. Taken off my guard, I still managed to express the shock and upset I had felt. However, I firmly told him that I could not let Barbara vet all my decisions.

Patrick seemed to have disappeared into thin air and was not in his office, yet again, the following morning. Suddenly Pat appeared to inform me of yet another meeting at 3 p.m. Her face expressed concern and she advised me to have someone of my choice in attendance for support.

I could have been knocked over by a feather at all these alarming calls to impromptu meetings. I did not have a clue who I could invite or why I should need support. The only people I could think of were Mrs Tonkin of the New Zealand

THE CATALYST NURSE

Nurses Association or Angela, a committee member of the church and tutor in gerontology at Christchurch College.

I rang Angela as I knew she would have some understanding of church procedures, and I was relieved when she agreed to attend. Meanwhile I experienced yet another long working day, when it was a challenge to focus on the tasks in hand due to the worry of an impending meeting.

Angela did not hide her surprise at the size of my dingy office. I told her I was celebrating as I had finally been given a telephone just the day before. Neil, accompanied by a man called Alex who I had never met, arrived for the meeting in my office. Tactless Neil did not introduce his companion and on spotting Angela told her she had no right to be at the meeting. Neil started the meeting by saying that, in the light of what I had said to him in the personnel office, he would have to ask for my resignation. Had he formulated that decision because I had said I would not let Barbara vet everything?

Alex was like a dictator as his harsh voice filled the room and he gesticulated wildly. His piercing stare gave me the sense he wished to turn me to stone, and he slammed his fists down on my desk. I feared he was about to thump me! His words were a blur to my frozen mind but he was saying something about not liking the way I worked, that I produced too much paperwork and documentation and any involvement with the Christchurch Health Department was not warranted. From now on I had to work under the agreement of Patrick and Barbara and if I could not accept this, I must resign by noon the following day! I was threatened that if I did not comply, things would get very nasty.

There was no opportunity for me to respond to the statements; Alex's whole demeanour was so overpowering.

I glanced at the white face of Angela, noticing her hands gripping the chair. I did a double take at Neil, who had tears running down his face. Alex suddenly stood up straight, pulled his jacket into position and marched out of the room, hesitantly followed by Neil.

Angela and I locked eyes in my now empty office; then she reached out to comfort me. My sobs were uncontrollable. The humiliation was overwhelming. Angela expressed her shock and disbelief at Neil's inappropriate behaviour in bringing the irrational Alex and all his bullying words to the meeting. Dazed, we both left the premises, having given ourselves time to try and gain enough composure to be able to drive home.

15. WHAT NEXT?

Things had moved so fast, there had been little hint of the cataclysm that was to erupt that day. It seemed unbelievable to arrive home to a world which knew nothing of the events of the past few hours. Everything was still going well for our move and, opening the door, I found Tom in a very happy mood.

'Hi Sue, guess who is coming tonight? We have two weeks to make up our minds if we want to have her.'

Tom held out a welcome home drink to me. My face must have revealed my distress. A mixture of sobs and spluttered words conveyed to Tom all that had occurred. I thought Tom was going to have a heart attack as the anger erupted throughout his whole body. I am sure he would have thumped Neil if he could!

Cursing Neil, Barbara and Patrick, he had obviously sussed out their motives. 'It is bullying, Sue, they don't want to help those poor old souls. They are frightened you will uncover more horror stories. They don't want to spend money to help those people.' Tom was stamping his feet and thumping the back of the chair. Frightened, Bobbie had run off down the hallway.

As was to be expected, Tom had an immediate plan for me along with much advice, informing me of my need to contact the union the next day. Tom did care, I knew that, and I

THE CATALYST NURSE

appreciated the cup of tea he went to brew, but I knew we would not sit down and discuss things together over our cups and saucers, but that we would sit down and he would tell me further what I must do and when.

I did not want to stir things but I suppose I did need Tom's wrath to encourage me to fight my corner. I agreed I would contact the New Zealand Nurses Association on the following day for advice.

I was surprised I slept at all but Bobbie offered his comfort by sleeping by my bed for the first time ever. I had silently wept throughout the night, which resulted in swollen eyes I decided to hide behind tinted glasses.

Five months since I had taken up my new post, 11th May 1984, was supposed to be our first introduction to our new family member, our little dog, but it was ruined by the stress that had overtaken our lives.

I tried to carry on at work as normally as possible. The elusive Patrick failed to be found in his office, yet again. I was grateful that I now had a telephone in my office. Contacting the New Zealand Nurses Association, I was told that they did not usually represent nurse managers. However, as this dispute was concerning patient care, they would be happy to help me. I also rang the health department and spoke to Mrs Belay, telling her of the problems with standards of care.

Just another day on automatic pilot. My new office phone startled me – I was not used to such a luxury of convenience. Pat had news for me – yes, another meeting! I was to attend Church House the following afternoon at 3 p.m. Just as Barbara had previously commented, Pat told me I was a good nurse. She went on to warn me that I should not take any rubbish from 'them'.

Words failed me yet again, although I would have appreciated a longer chat with Pat – it would have been so comforting to have the views of a fellow Englishwoman on all that was going on, although I guessed her hands were tied in terms of her saying anything further.

I returned home to further interrogation by Tom; my mind was numb. Dear Bobbie sensed my stress, always ensuring he was by my side. Tom, likewise, found his way to try and distract me and must have felt disappointed in my lack of interest in the Torvill and Dean tickets he produced; usually I would have been over the moon about such an opportunity.

16. DESOLATION

Even the traffic seemed to be against me as I drove to work the following day, butterflies fluttering in my stomach. I recognised the need to concentrate as I had a couple of near misses, just minor affairs needing the warning pips of car horns and one to awaken me to the fact the traffic lights now indicated go.

Arriving at work, I was grateful for an immediate start and responded to an urgent message from Eden Hospital. A patient had passed away, and the relatives had arrived to strip the room, literally. All the hospital belongings, including curtains and bedding, had been taken. Verbal abuse had been hurled down the phone at the sister when she tried to ask for the return of the hospital property.

I advised that in future a member of staff should supervise family members but, on this occasion, there was not much else we could do.

My mind had been nicely distracted during this little saga, but once everything was sorted I had time to dwell on the forthcoming meeting. My dark office offered little comfort so I decided to pop home to prepare for the afternoon battlefield.

Dear old Bobbie greeted me, faithful as ever, his tail wagging ten to the dozen. My tears soaked his coat as I sat with him for a cuddle.

THE CATALYST NURSE

A good old pot of English tea somehow made me feel a little better before I took a quick shower and chose my blue suit; power dressing always helped my confidence. I decided on no mascara for obvious reasons! Tears were not my usual style but lately I had shed floods of the things. I was shocking myself with all this emotion; where had my normal British stiff upper lip disappeared to? I had been made of steel as I faced so many difficult situations during my 18-year nursing career and, as you will imagine, while working on the accident and emergency wards I had dealt with some dreadful injuries and fatalities.

All these aggressive meetings had sucked the soul out of me. I knew, for the first time in my life, I was waiting for the straw that would break the camel's back. The drip, drip, drip of resistance to the work I was trying to do to improve the lifestyle of residents and patients was pooling into a reservoir about to break its banks.

I focussed my mind away from these unhelpful thoughts and organised my briefcase so that I would be able to retrieve any supporting documents without hesitation, whatever they surprised me with. I was going into battle fully armed, and a parting lick from Bobbie was the armour I needed as I left to face the group who seemed to be determined on becoming my enemy.

I felt relieved that Mrs Tonkin was meeting me at the entrance to Church House to accompany me to the meeting. She had insisted, 'We will go into the meeting together, that way you will feel supported and I will have the pleasure of meeting this caring group of Christians.' The sarcasm in her voice was noticeable. Mrs Tonkin boosted my ego by commenting on my professional appearance and I admired her mint-green suit, feeling proud to have a smart woman to accompany me as we strode up the stairs together.

Pat's friendly smile welcomed us as we reached the top of the flight of steps, and I was warmed by her effort to calm me as she gave my hand a squeeze.

The room was not as hot as before as the sun had passed to the opposite side of the building, so at least I would not appear flustered with a red face. It felt humiliating to see Neil, Barbara and Patrick sat huddled together as the terrible threesome they had become. 'Three against one' seemed to be their message.

Angela, wearing a floral dress, stood up and walked towards us as we entered. She shook both our hands and I could read the message in her eyes – although she was on the church board, she was here to support me. I tried to sit in an assertive but comfortable position.

Neil had chosen a smart outfit too; we were playing the same game of power dressing, no doubt. I quite admired his sports jacket, white shirt and pale-blue tie with light trousers and suede shoes.

Lacking in etiquette as was often the case, Neil blundered into an awkward introductory speech claiming he had given enough time already to this problem. He did not appear to register the offence I felt by his reference to me as 'a problem'. His wish to rapidly resolve the problem reminded me so much of the night-time tour he had originally led, where I was rushed around as if there was no tomorrow. His insult had taken my mind away from the rest of his ramblings but I just caught the words, 'We have come to an impasse and I want a solution.'

Angela jumped in at that point, defending me. She demanded to know why a principal nurse should be treated so shabbily when she was fulfilling her job description to an excellent standard. I couldn't help but think maybe too excellently for their liking as it reflected their weaknesses.

Mrs Tonkin told the group she had spoken to Mrs Brown, the principal nurse at the hospital where I had previously worked, and that she had given me a good reference. She explained that I was known to speak straight from the shoulder but was never rude.

I studied their faces for their reactions. Yes, it was true I spoke my mind but nurses needed to be honest and as a senior nurse I had to speak with authority. I noticed Patrick and Barbara sneaking looks at each other, which it seemed was the way they were able to understand each other.

Neil had been shuffling uncomfortably in his chair as they spoke in my defence and support. He tried to sway things by turning the fault on me, saying that the impasse was the result of my failure to listen to Patrick or Barbara.

Barbara, resembling Cruella de Vil with her unusual hairstyle and scheming ways, slinked forward and told me I had already received two warnings.

Her lies swirled around her but I had been given inner strength and calm by the lovely words of Angela and Mrs Tonkin, so I also leant forward, mirroring Barbara's action. My voice came out low but piercing: 'That is purely superfluous!' Afterwards, I was not sure why I chose that word, I wasn't sure if it was the correct word, but the tone, confidence and brevity of my reply seemed to have done the trick as Cruella, sorry Barbara, looked astonished and pulled her chair back so that she was out of my view, hidden by Patrick.

I observed Patrick preparing to speak but my self-respect had risen to such a height that I cut him dead by speaking first: 'I really don't want to have any more to do with you.'

Silence fell. One could have heard the proverbial pin drop.

I felt Mrs Tonkin's hand on my shoulder. 'Do you mean you are leaving?' she asked gently.

'Yes, I will go,' I said in a haze, having come to my own conclusion — what was the point in working for people like these?

Looking downward and bent slightly forward, Patrick and Barbara couldn't leave the room fast enough.

Last time it had been tears from the hypocritical Neil; this time it was whispered words of shame: 'I'm so sorry.'

Mrs Tonkin stood up, asking Neil if they could discuss the events of this meeting in his office. Angela and I sat in silence for about half an hour, as if turned to stone by the icy hearts we had just experienced. Angela put a comforting hand on my arm but speech would not come to either of us. Eventually, Mrs Tonkin returned with Neil, who was stuttering out some sort of regret, which I felt added further insult.

Mrs Tonkin offered to drive me home, which sounded like a wise decision. She assured me I would receive a reference and three months' salary, but none of that mattered to me right then and it felt degrading to even be discussing such issues. Even she did not seem to realise the inappropriateness of her conversation at this moment in time, as she continued chatting, saying she had been asked to choose my replacement and that a lot of good would come out of all this. Yes, my downfall was to be the uplift of others! None of that helped just now. On and on she went, telling me the problems were Neil and Patrick, who could never agree on things, as if I did not know that already. I just didn't listen to what she then decided to list as Barbara's problem; I could have told her a hundred of Barbara's problems!

17. THE UNTROD SNOW OF THE FUTURE

Tom's reactions to the outcome were predictable – he was so angry. Poor Bobbie ran off in fear, again. Tom eventually calmed down enough to suggest we eat out at a café, realising I was not in a suitable state to prepare dinner. I found I had no appetite but tried to eat an omelette as I knew my body needed nourishment.

The next day I tried to maintain some sort of routine, taking Bobbie to Hagley Park. The sun did its best to cheer me as did the host of daffodils and tremendous tulip display.

The Torvill and Dean Ice Spectacular had come at an appropriate time. Somehow I summoned the strength to attend. As one would expect, the stadium was packed. They had to condense their performance down to solely bolero due to Christopher Dean's strained back muscle – I could relate.

As the music started, it induced feelings of nostalgia and I felt a longing for the success I had hoped to bring to my vocation. Bolero always ended with the volume reaching as loud a crescendo as possible, which, on this occasion, invoked in me emotions of anger with the people who had stolen my soul. I needed to find a way to regain it.

Tom acknowledged the stress of the previous weeks had taken a terrible toll on us both, and he insisted that we stay at home to recover. He sold the idea to me by reminding me that as Anna, our new puppy, was soon to arrive, it would be a good opportunity to prepare for her. We expected some problems because Anna had spent six years in kennels and we doubted she would be house-trained. Time off would also mean we could concentrate on the house move.

However, I soon discovered Tom's true motives because he was arranging for us to find a solicitor on Monday morning, regardless of my wishes on the matter. He explained that the church had led me up the garden path, allowing me to take on a mortgage, telling me that I was doing well in everyone's eyes, that they were all happy with me. They had then construed events to stop me discovering even more unacceptable practices. Tom had decided that we should take the church to court so that the media would become aware and the terrible conditions would become public knowledge. However, I did not want the press involved because I would be seen as breaking confidentiality and would therefore never be able to nurse again.

Tom was not prepared to listen to my point of view on the matter. He wanted retribution. I wished he would go to work and leave me in peace to gather my thoughts, but that wasn't to be and he nagged me to seek legal advice, so I agreed to ring Mrs Tonkin for guidance. She let me know that my previous manager from the health department, Angela and herself were all happy to support me but would have to withdraw if I went to a solicitor. She informed me that Neil was holding another meeting, a mass one where he planned

THE CATALYST NURSE

to explain any misunderstandings about my exit. I think he owed me that explanation!

Mrs Tonkin said Angela had told her I was a catalyst and my leaving spontaneously would spur the church into action. In time, I might come to appreciate that but for now it meant little to me. I had wanted nothing more than to make positive changes to the quality of life for my residents, but I had never dreamt this desire would be achieved through my own sacrifice. She also let me know that Angela was going to remain on the council, where she would be more effective. I really did feel like the sacrificial lamb.

I concluded our chat by letting Mrs Tonkin know I wished to leave the matter in her capable hands for now, and of course I thanked her greatly.

Almost in the same instant the receiver clicked back onto its cradle, the phone rang again. It was Mrs Brown. She was very empathetic to my situation and offered me a sister's post immediately. Of course I was flattered, but I just could not entertain the thought – I was too broken to think straight.

After a light lunch, yet again the telephone made me jump. Daphne wanted to know all the details and I listened with frustration to someone else telling me what a good nurse I was and how I did not deserve this treatment. Such well-meant words, at this stage, just made things worse because if it was true, if I was such a valued professional and if they all thought I had been treated unfairly, why was nobody doing anything about it? All I could do was sit and stare into space, my mind in turmoil. I was too mentally and physically exhausted to be on my guard against further manipulation by

Tom, who seemed to be taking a dislike to Mrs Tonkin who now explained Neil could not hold his mass meeting as he had not received my letter of resignation.

Mrs Tonkin had apparently come to the conclusion that maybe there *had* been a breach of my contract. I mulled over my letter of resignation, deciding to follow my usual policy of being brief and to the point. 'After the meeting I attended on Friday 11th May 1984, I have no alternative but to give you my resignation. Yours sincerely, Susan Lauri.'

Tom posted it at the main post office so they would receive it the following morning.

Antony, a member of the church council, requested to see me the following Friday. Everything became a jumble over the next few days. Daphne rang near midnight after Neil's mass meeting, delivering yet more of the same: so many people at the meeting had declared how wrongly I had been treated, all singing my praises. Daphne said that I should get a solicitor.

I appreciated Tom doing the shopping the next day while I found some me time to collect my thoughts. I had got to the stage where I could not stand any noise or sudden movements, so the ringing phone made me nearly jump out of my skin – Pat this time. I was surprised to hear Patrick was off work himself and could only see this as a cowardly action to escape the fallout. She said Pat, the sister in charge of the hospital, had expressed concern that her own uncooperative attitude had led to my resignation. All I could think was, *Why did all these people not come out of the woodwork before it was too late?*

The tales continued. At the committee meeting a church adviser had suggested the council clean up the homes and hospital, keeping quiet, and I would go away! Another member of the council was going to question all staff about their opinion of my management style. I wanted people to stop poking their noses into my business; it was all too late to help and I felt like some sort of celebrity hounded by unwanted attention.

Tom was just as bad. Returning with the shopping, he was straight on the phone to a Mr Palmer. As soon as he had put the receiver down, he was full of the fact that this Mr Palmer had advised that we had a good case against the church for constructive dismissal. I wanted to scream to the world to leave me alone but Tom refused to return to work, saying he did not think I could cope without him, although, in reality, I knew he was worried I might do something he did not approve of regarding the case.

Before I knew it Friday was here and the visit of Antony. Of course, Tom beat me to the door. Antony was a man in his early 40s, medium height and build, balding dark hair and a round cheery face. His eyes gave an impression of sincerity and he still had a European demeanour, in my opinion. I could remember seeing him at my first board meeting.

While drinking coffee, Antony talked of his conversations with Angela and Mrs Tonkin, expressing his amazement when informed of what had been taking place without the board's knowledge. He told me that he and several other members of the board had expressed their delight at having a nurse of such quality, and were looking forward to the improvements to their homes and hospital. Antony was also horrified to learn of the dismissal of my predecessor, who had been paid off. This lady had received a lot of respect from the church council and community in general for the many years of hard work she had given to the homes and hospital. She had achieved a great deal, forming a large group of voluntary supporters. These volunteers helped maintain the homes and support the patients and residents. It appeared to be déjà vu – the pattern of my story seemed to follow hers. The volunteers had diminished since her resignation over a year before, prior to my appointment.

Antony told me of a time before my appointment when $1,000 had gone missing from Eden House. He concluded his visit by saying himself and other members of the board felt a grave error had occurred and would I consider returning if asked.

My 'No' could not have been clearer.

18. WAKING UP TIRED

Exhaustion enveloped my entire being. Noise, noise, noise was everywhere. Tom, as usual, was shouting and ranting about the way I had been treated. He moaned about my professionalism, forbidding me from taking on litigation. He kept going on about the poor standard of care of the elderly in the church homes – as if I did not remember! It was as if he wasn't listening to me. Bobbie hid constantly behind the lounge door, shaking.

Everything seemed to annoy Tom – for example, the shops didn't stock the things he wanted and he couldn't find any of his favourite Imperial Leather soap and shaving lotion on the shelves. As I loathed the smell of it, I was secretly pleased.

Sometimes I had the impression Tom would have liked me to return to work for Church House, but I knew how unprofessional the staff were and there was now no room for trust, so it just wasn't possible.

A two-hour lunch with Antony and Angela at a local restaurant later that week felt productive. Despite my constant weariness, I had managed to pass on information about the care, or lack of it, in the respective establishments. Further meetings had been taking place at Church House but when I enquired, Angela and Antony would only say they were closed meetings. Daphne rang later the same day, speaking kindly with great empathy and giving me the name of a solicitor. However, remembering how friendly Daphne had become with Neil I tried to be careful with any information I had, which was very little.

Life gradually began to return to normal, probably because Tom had returned to work, giving me the mental space I needed. His boss suggested the next time a visit to Wellington came up on Tom's itinerary, he should take me with him at the firm's expense!

Ever since my resignation had become public knowledge, the telephone rang continually with calls from interested people – the local press and general busybodies. This caused me great agitation so I eventually disconnected the phone.

Opening the front door one morning to take Bobbie for his walk, I found myself faced with a reporter and photographer who had his hand raised and finger poised about to ring the bell. He seized the opportunity to take a photograph. Bobbie instantly turned into a vicious guard dog, leaping up at the man with a camera and gripping his arm as neighbours ran to see what all the kerfuffle was about. I felt Tom was to blame for all this media attention – he had sought it out.

A freelance journalist, who was successful in having her articles printed in popular magazines, contacted me and offered to write an article. This lady who told me to call her Robin was persistent. After about an hour of persuasive conversation with her, I realised that other members of the church had been in contact and were talking to her. Finally, I agreed to read the article that Robin intended to write, giving my opinion on its contents, strongly stipulating I did not wish to be involved or mentioned in any way.

Robin, who was certainly assertive, explained her personal motives for wanting to write such an article, saying she was shocked by the rumours of the living conditions of both residents and patients. She was concerned for the caring people who worked in these homes for very low pay and in poor working conditions. She left me a copy of her article and I found it was a very balanced piece of work with an overall view comparing and contrasting Butlers Court to Eden House and Hospital. She discussed the socioeconomic class of both, their financial differences and the legal implications to the care of the elderly.

There were several pictures of Daphne, who freely gave her perspective on elderly care. This made me wonder if Daphne had been the instigator of the article; she certainly wasn't shy when it came to publicity. However, Robin would not say where she had acquired the initial information or who she had been speaking to. Robin was well aware of the poor state of Eden House and the substandard care for patients in the hospital. It was obvious she had visited Butlers Court, as she described how the decor had captivated her imagination with its colourful furnishings. The passages relating to Eden House were much shorter. Robin quoted remarks made by residents who were really too poor to live anywhere else. A retired health visitor was quoted as saying she was grateful to have a roof over her head.

Tom agreed it was a very well-written piece of work; however, he felt Robin should have included the way I had been treated by the church. Once again, in complete contrast to how I felt about the matter, Tom believed his opinion was the correct one. I was determined that the article would contain no reference to me.

Finally, it was the day for the arrival of Anna, our seven-year-old West Highland terrier. At first, Bobbie and Anna were wary of each other. Bobbie was quiet, obedient and loving whereas Anna was feral, having lived in breeding kennels all her life with no discipline, and she certainly had a self-reliant personality. Bobbie loved a cuddle but Anna did not like having any personal contact with humans, wriggling out of any offered hugs.

Tom's controlling nature seemed to be getting worse, and he told me it was my job to house-train Anna. I saw through his manipulation as he tried to blind me with talk about the moving date for the new house, claiming we might be able to move in earlier than expected. He then just slipped into the conversation that my reference had arrived in the post that day.

I was furious that he had opened my post. He tried to change the conversation by saying how the New Zealand system of postboxes at the end of the drive was not as good as letters through your door.

I was not falling for his tactics, and when he realised that, he moodily drew the letter from inside his briefcase and threw it at me!

There were two letters from Neil. One requested the return of any documents I had. There was a cheque for three months' salary, which Tom snatched from my hand at the same time as claiming he would take my briefcase and lock it in the boot of his car as our solicitor would need those documents, not Neil. The second letter was the reference.

To whom it may concern,

This is to certify that Susan Lauri was employed by this agency as principal nurse for a period of five months, from January 1984 until her resignation in May 1984.
I have no hesitation in testifying to her efficiency as a nurse and to her high standards in every aspect of patient care. During her time with us, she was conscientious and hard-working, highly motivated and reliable. During her stay, she exercised a high degree of supervision and initiated programmes of training and change.
I commend her for any position requiring a high degree of advanced nursing skills.

Neil Thompson
Director of Church services.

I could have choked on Neil's hypocrisy and Tom's deceit and manipulation. At that moment, there was only room in my heart for Bobbie and Anna.

19. THINGS GO ON AND ON

I began to think I should play Tom at his own game by not telling him everything, and I secretly went back to Eden Hospital one night to return my keys. I purposefully parked my car out of sight and entered when I knew the staff would be busy. I noted there were still unpleasant smells. I left my labelled keys on the desk of the charge nurse.

Tom had organised everything for the move but I felt forlorn that he was leaving me to things on the actual day.

'The removal men will be early so I hope you have everything ready!' Tom was dressed and about to leave for work. 'The agent told me the keys to the new house are in the front door. You need to leave the keys to this house in the back of the front door, so the door only has to be pushed open,' he continued in an assertive voice.

I felt so alone. All excitement had evaporated. I was still easily moved to tears. The removal men arrived at 8:30 a.m. and by 10 a.m. they were ready to move all our belongings to the new house at Halswell, Christchurch. It would have felt a much happier experience if Tom had been with me.

As if I had not got enough to do on my removal day, the phone rang just as we entered the new property. The caller was Mrs Tonkin from the Nurses Association. She reiterated once more that she did not usually support nurse managers but, as this case was to do with patient care, her boss had agreed she must help me. The ongoing belated comments of praise were sounding very much like a broken record. She said how well I had performed in my job, especially given the circumstances. She surprised me with her new interjection that she would like to take my case to the bishop. I found myself agreeing to the meeting Mrs Tonkin arranged.

I felt very nervous on the day we were to meet this high-ranking man of God. Suddenly wondering how one addressed a bishop, I went for 'Sir'.

The Reverend Peters, Bishop of Christchurch, was a middle-aged man of great maturity. He spoke softly during introductions and we felt comfortable in his presence, which emulated a state of serenity. I felt calm sat among the various artefacts in his office.

The bishop listened intently as Mrs Tonkin explained my situation to him. It was difficult to read his thoughts but he did appear very sanctimonious when my resignation was mentioned. As our meeting progressed, the initial sense of calm slowly evaporated and we did not recognise sincerity in his weak handshake and lack of eye contact as he ended our meeting. We felt mildly satisfied by his closing promise that he would look into the matter.

Sitting together in my car after the meeting, Mrs Tonkin and I discussed our thoughts. We both agreed the bishop was clearly a well-practised negotiator. Mrs Tonkin was still unwilling to involve herself with a solicitor, which was understandable as it would have threatened her career, but I was in a different boat and said, 'If it is the end of my career but it means these people get better care, then it will have been worth it.'

Life was a waiting game over the next few weeks and I do not know what I would have done without the distraction, love and companionship of Anna and Bobbie. Our new house was a dream and folk back home would not have believed the quarter-of-an-acre-sized plot on which our home stood.

Our three extra-large bedrooms meant we had plenty of space for guests. A sense of luxury was created by the wall-to-ceiling windows. The pretty gardens surrounded our large swimming pool, set in a terracotta tiled patio. I knew that our English friends would have died for our large, modern kitchen with its central island. The open-plan design contributed to the light and airy ambience.

The massive garage could house three cars. The whole picture of our new home would have been unbelievable to us back in the days of our Cornish lifestyle.

I did find our cul-de-sac to be a dormitory road due to the fact that the neighbours were out at work all day and nobody was around to make us feel at home. Of course, I could fill my days by swimming, unpacking, gardening but I lacked a sense of purpose, which added to my growing sense of melancholy. I took up tapestry, which I did as I sat in front of the television watching reruns of my favourite British programmes.

Tom's work commitments took him away for days at a time, which added to my growing sense of loneliness. On the other hand, I appreciated my distance from his rantings about the church situation. He had left me with strict instructions not to talk to anyone about the situation. On the evenings he was home, I enjoyed a swim in the pool to escape his mutterings as he listened to his music in the lounge.

The microwave was a new experience for us and I enjoyed experimenting with recipes. *Georgie would be impressed* I thought as I tried to copy the chocolate cake my sister had once made for us. My resulting rubber creation bounced across the lawn when I tried to feed it to the birds before Tom could see my disaster and tell me what I had done wrong. I did not need his haughty explanation that I had not allowed for the cooking to continue once removed from the microwave.

My spirits were low; I guess boredom was trying to rear its ugly head. I was never a person to suffer from that trait, so it was just another thing to fight against in the increasing temperature.

Sleep was not always my friend, so I was not pleased to be awoken by our dogs barking one morning at 3 a.m. I wondered if my medication was responsible for the impression that our king-size bed was rocking and our curtains were doing a jig. A picture decided to fall from the wall and I guessed this was a sign I was not coping mentally.

Relieved, as you might have guessed we were in the midst of a mini earthquake! I did know that Canterbury and Christchurch, and South Island in particular, were susceptible to earth movements. Canterbury is situated on the Alpine Fault, which runs almost the entire length of the Southern Alps between the Pacific and Australian tectonic plates. Mini quakes were not uncommon.

Rushing down to rescue our dogs, I nearly slipped on the floor, realising the shocked creatures had, understandably, each experienced a little accident! Bobbie and Anna were my life and their safety was the only thing that mattered to me.

The patio doors would no longer glide open due to structural damage and the pool had spilt its contents. Clearing up the after-effects of our first experience of an earthquake would at least give me a worthwhile task in the morning.

Sue swimming.

20. FINDING THE WILL TO FIND THE WAY

I could not believe it was three months since I had left my position. Living in our new house brought larger bills to our door and I was aware that finances were tight. I had been disappointed that all six of the applications I had made for nursing positions in Christchurch had brought no positive response – I guess news travels fast.

As a nurse, I recognised in myself the signs of depression. Anxiety and loneliness were consuming me and I would lay in bed, finding no reason to get up. I found myself fixating on the postbox, hoping a letter from my mother had been popped in. I felt like Bobbie and Anna, waiting at the door for the return of their human. I wrote more frequently to my mum but I would not tell her of my problems, and as I wasn't doing much with my time it was difficult to find suitable content.

I realised that I had better see the doctor concerning my increasing melancholy. I was not in the least surprised to be prescribed antidepressants. They seemed to help and, feeling slightly stronger, I eventually accepted a post back at the midwifery department where I had previously worked before Tom's great idea to change my life.

It wasn't long before I took over the antenatal clinic, my medication helping me to focus. This involved me organising parentcraft classes and lectures on relevant subjects. I enjoyed the interaction with the couples, a mixture of people of Caucasian and Māori origin. I found that the Caucasian couples liked to sit formally on chairs facing the speaker, while the Māori couples preferred to relax on beanbags, happily chatting to one another.

I commenced my lecture by progressing through the various types of contraception, stating the advantages and disadvantages of each method. Personally, I found the Caucasians, who were mostly European, revealed a reserved attitude while the Māori participants appeared uninhibited. I always found it difficult not to blush when discussing condoms. At one session, holding up a condom, I began to explain the correct way to wear one. Trying to disperse the air of embarrassment, I asked if there were any volunteers who would be willing to demonstrate. The European men blushed and looked at their feet.

'Missy, I will help you,' said a Māori man sitting on a beanbag in front of me, his hand on his trouser zip! The group erupted into laughter, especially as the man's wife went on to tell everyone about the different flavours she liked and that bumpy ones were best!

I did not know where to look and declined his kind offer, using my fingers instead to show the now very amused and relaxed group that one needed to leave space at the end of the condom for fluid. A movement of air from the fans I had put in place to cool us all agitated the end of the condom. Convulsions of laughter could be heard from the audience. Comments came thick and fast but I don't think you will want me to repeat them here! I was still smiling to myself about the evening's events when, clearing the room after the meeting, a student nurse who had been assisting me laughed and said, 'Only the English could keep a straight face under such circumstances!'

The laughter had been excellent medicine for me and I was glad I had returned to my department. I dared to hope I was getting better.

Things had quietened concerning the legal battle Tom was contemplating and the interview with the bishop, so I guess the lack of worry in those areas had also helped my healing process. The bishop had said he would reserve any opinion until after discussing the matter with the director. I knew Neil was away in America.

I was wary that Mrs Tonkin might prefer to calm the situation rather than be proactive, so I decided to drop a line to the bishop. Was I turning into Tom doing things like this?

Dear Sir,

With reference to our meeting with Mrs Tonkin, I would like to thank you for the time you spent with us.
I believe Neil Thompson, the director, will have returned from his American visit.
I look forward to hearing from you regarding enquires made and actions taken on the following matters we discussed:
1 Events regarding my enforced resignation
2 Patient and resident care in the church's homes and hospital

THE CATALYST NURSE

3 The mismanagement by administrative staff
I look forward to an early reply.

Yours faithfully,
Susan Lauri SRN, SCM, DND

I was aware, again, that Tom was meddling with my post when he sarcastically mentioned I had post from the bishop. I had noticed he had even taken it upon himself to open the letters from my mum. Snatching my own post from his hand I read:

Dear Mrs Lauri,

Thank you for your letter of July referring to our meeting in June. I was glad to meet you and spend time discussing the situation with you and Mrs Tonkin.
I have made some enquires regarding your resignation, patient and resident care in the church homes and hospital and about the administration practices involved.
As I explained to you on the occasion of our discussion, it would not be possible for me to take action regarding your personal situation. The Committee of the Council of the Church has reviewed the matter and endorsed the actions already taken by the director.
I can, however, assure you that steps have been taken to establish a staff committee which will have major responsibility relating to all matters leading to the appointment of new staff members and also will be involved in any measures involving

the termination of appointments of staff members. The Committee of the Council has taken active steps to look into the matters concerning the quality of care and to ensure that it will match the needs of the residents in the various homes and the hospital.
I am glad to have had discussion with you and can assure you that we trust that there will be beneficial results from the unfortunate situation in which you found yourself.

With every good wish,
Bishop of Christchurch.

Tom jumped straight in before I could gather my thoughts, instructing me that I needed a solicitor. I wanted to digest the letter, which, in my opinion, did contain some positives to celebrate – things might get better for the residents as a result of my experiences.

The sound of the ritual of a morning cup of tea being placed on my bedside locker woke me from a fretful sleep. Why had I bothered the bishop? I had reignited my feelings of melancholy, and Tom's controlling ways were creeping back again.

Tom was dressed ready for work but it was still quite early in the morning. 'Listen, Sue, can you hear me?' He spoke sharply. 'You have an appointment with a David Mason this morning at 11 a.m. I will take you there but you must catch the bus back home. I can't trust you to drive in the state you have been in lately.'

So, he had noticed my depression was worsening again. Drowsily I tried to make sense of what he had just said but his voice was still droning on.

'A look around the shops and a coffee afterwards will be a change for you.'

I recognised this as one of his manipulative tricks to try and bribe me to go through with this appointment he had made without asking me. I felt like throwing the cup of tea over him as he continued with his plan. 'I've got your briefcase with all you need in it. So, make yourself look presentable. I will be back to pick you up at 10.15. Don't forget to take the dogs for their early walk.'

Obediently, I was ready when he popped back from work to escort me to the offices of David Mason & Brothers, Barristers and Solicitors. I wondered how much the fees were going to be in this expensive-looking establishment with its glass-walled offices. I was greeted by a friendly young woman in her early 20s who led me to meet David Mason, a much younger man than I had expected. I looked into his twinkling eyes and felt at ease when he told me his grandfather had originated from Birmingham, England. I found him very attentive as I shared my story and did not mind him making so many notes. Politely, he thanked me for telling him all about my five-month post. His manner was reassuring and, after clarifying a few points, he said there was definitely a case to answer and he would be happy to help me find a satisfactory conclusion.

I felt he understood my desire to help the poor neglected residents who lived in shocking circumstances with no standard of care and very little dignity. I shared with David that Tom felt the only way I could ensure some improvement to their care was to take the church to court so the world would know just how bad life was for the residents and patients in church care. I was aware that it may ruin my career but I could not live with myself if I did nothing.

David closed our meeting by accepting the files I had brought with me and he promised an early written acceptance of my case. My exhaustion had returned by the time I left his office.

Gate to the house where the dogs barked.

Street view of the house.

21. TRAUMA

The caffè latte had never tasted better and gave me time to regain my composure, although the experience of talking to a solicitor hadn't been as traumatic as I had feared. Not being much of a shopper, browsing a few gift shops and window-shopping for clothes soon bored me. I decided to look for the bus stop, and the timetable revealed I had another 20 minutes to wait.

A beautiful sunny day offered a sense of hope so I felt it would be pleasant to sit on the covered bench by the stop, to relax and admire the beautiful cathedral opposite. Whether it was the heat of the sun on the glass shelter, my pent-up emotions or a spiritual experience as I admired the place of worship, I do not know, but I was suddenly aware of flowing water and voices asking if I was all right. It turned out I was crying uncontrollably and shaking as if I was about to have a convulsion. Was it a panic attack? I did not know why I was suddenly running away from all the Good Samaritans at the bus stop, shouting at them to leave me alone.

I found myself cowering away in a narrow alleyway as I let my tears flow. Self-loathing flooded over me as I plopped down on black bin bags full of rubbish. Eventually, I managed to find the strength of mind to force myself to return to the bus stop. I had a real need to get home. I was relieved to see a bus had transported the earlier passengers away; I would have felt humiliated to see them again. I was desperate to arrive home before Tom, to get some peace before all his interrogations began. I could imagine all the questions already: 'What did he say?', 'How did it go?', 'Does he think we will be successful?', 'You did leave the documents with him, didn't you?'

I arrived home to the incessant barking of my dogs. I checked around the property as I now knew Bobbie was a secret guard dog. Already an emotional wreck, the sight of two uniformed men behind the gates was nearly enough to finish me off.

They introduced themselves as members of the New Zealand Animal Rescue Association. My muddled mind managed to understand from their garble that one of our neighbours had complained about our dogs, who apparently barked all day long. I was surprised for various reasons, one being that I was not aware of any neighbours who were home in the day. I wondered why they had not waited to share a friendly concern with us before going straight to the authorities.

The men must have seen my distressed state because they tried to calm things by saying that now they had seen the dogs they were satisfied they were well cared for. However, my anxieties flew sky-high again, when they then went on to suggest I should have Anna's tongue cut out as she was a constant chatterer. If they received any more complaints further action would be taken!

The evening air had an uncommon chill about it, possibly due to the heavy breeze, but it matched my sense of impending doom. Pulling on a cardigan, I took the dogs to the park, where I came across a stout man who, on seeing me, marched directly over. Bracing myself for some sort of confrontation, I did not offer a friendly greeting. I took him to be a nosey neighbour when he claimed he had seen the animal welfare officers. However, I later felt ashamed when I realised he was doing me a big favour when he went on to tell me he had seen two young sons of another neighbour pushing sticks through the gates to torment the dogs. I understood immediately why the dogs had been barking their heads off.

The days passed in a blur as I worried how things were going on the legal front. One evening over supper, Tom was in one of his silent moods but I knew him well enough to wonder what this was an omen of.

We finished our coffees, and I was sitting down to watch the television when Tom pulled out two large brown envelopes from his pocket and pushed them along the sofa to me. A letter from the solicitor engaged by the church to our solicitor set my heart racing as I read of their concern at the wide-ranging and damaging allegations. They were considering the possibility of a meeting. Feeling sick with worry, I found the sense of mounting tension unbearable. I asked myself if we had stirred a ginormous hornets' nest.

The second letter was from my solicitor informing me of the decision of the church, which was to advise him there was to be no further action from them. The solicitor had attached a further letter, from himself, informing me that if the matter was to be continued we must issue a writ.

Speechless, I looked at Tom's sly face as he confessed, 'I spoke to this solicitor chap, he rang while you were out.' His tone was hard and cold.

'And the letters?' I whispered. Even my anger had lost its energy. I could see no point in raving about Tom opening my mail; we had spoken of this many times. It made me feel violated.

'They were in the postbox, you must have forgotten to collect them,' Tom said flippantly.

I stood and left the room to take my darlings on yet another walk – anything to get away from this robotic existence.

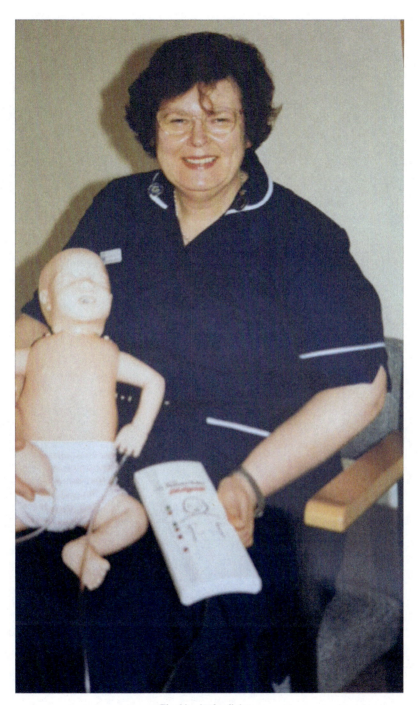

Teaching in the clinic.

The dogs.

The dogs.

Dogs in the bath.

22. MORE MUDDLES

I appreciated working on night duty, just myself and another midwife. There was so much to do, we had little time for chat. I was learning the truth of the saying 'A dog is a man's best friend' as I withdrew into myself, feeling let down by so many people. Anna and Bobbie were truly my lifelines. One of the older midwives on day duty was close to members of the church and if there was a quiet moment she would castigate me to a point of rudeness. Nothing I did was right in her eyes.

Back at our house, whereas once I had longed for post, hopefully from Mum, I now lived in dread of the contents of the postbox, and it often seemed to be bulging these days.

Noticing the postbox was full as I returned from a morning dog walk, I was pleased to find Mum's familiar handwriting on the airmail envelope. A dreaded A4 envelope stood out among the rest with the solicitor's title stamped on the back. I needed a pot of coffee before I dared to open it. At least I had got to it before Tom!

I reread it several times, trying to digest its contents. The four major paragraphs that stuck out for me were:

On 14th May Mrs Lauri tendered a form of resignation. That resignation was tendered, however, only after it had been made plain to Mrs Lauri that you no longer wished her to do the job for which she had been employed and only because of the extreme pressure put on her to resign. We are of the view that, in these circumstances, Mrs Lauri's 'resignation' was in reality a constructive dismissal.

In the weeks prior to the termination of Mrs Lauri's employment, various reasons were given to justify the pressure on her to resign. After examining each of the reasons, it is apparent to us that the aspects of Mrs Lauri's conduct complained of were either directly covered by her job description or were professional nursing practice of ethics. As such, they could not amount to a proper reason for terminating Mrs Lauri's employment and we can only conclude that her dismissal was wrongful.

When Mrs Lauri left your employ, she was given a sum of money equivalent to three months' salary. At that time, no one knew what the effect would be on Mrs Lauri's career and professional reputation of the sudden termination of her employment as principal nurse. Clearly all parties hoped that the effect would be minimal. In fact, the effect has been substantial. As a direct result of the timing and manner of termination of employment with you, she has been unable to obtain a position of equal or even comparable status. After three months of searching for another position, Mrs Lauri was compelled by financial pressures to accept the best job available, being that of a staff midwife at Burwood Hospital. In having to take that position, she has suffered a substantial drop in salary, is obliged to work shifts and unsociable hours, and has to travel a substantial distance. So far as the effect on Mrs Lauri's career is concerned, it is presently estimated that a termination of her employment with you will set her back three to four years.

On this basis, we are of the view that Mrs Lauri has a course of action open to her. Before advising her to take formal steps, however, we believe it is only proper to acquaint you with our conclusions and invite both your comments on those conclusions and any proposals you may wish to make on an informal basis.

Having finished off my pot of coffee, I asked myself what I thought of all this. At least I could collect and process my own thoughts on the contents before Tom had the chance to brainwash me. So, what were my thoughts? *Oh God do I have to go through all this? I've just got my old job back and the antidepressants are starting to take effect. I don't need this in my life.*

I began to shake, then the convulsions began again. I could hear the coffee mug shaking on the table but could not see anything for the rain running over my eyes. I knew Tom would be pleased but I was reticent. I hoped I could hold on to my clarity of thought once he started taking charge.

I felt I had achieved all that I had wanted for the residents because I had made the health department aware of the poor situation at the houses and hospital. The church was now aware of their poor care. All of Christchurch now had a low opinion of them as carers for the elderly. Patrick was no longer in post, although I didn't know if he had retired, been pushed or just changed departments. Lynda had suffered a nervous breakdown and was replaced.

I believed Tom's main motive was to gain financially. Sadly, though, the financial settlement he desired would come from the contributions of parishioners meant for the relief of the poor and destitute. Unlike Tom, I would be quite happy with a public apology rather than receiving any money.

As I had feared, Tom was ecstatic on reading the solicitor's letter. I tried not to cringe when he gave me a big hug and kiss before I left for work that night.

Taking my turn on the labour ward, I arrived to a quiet shift with just one mother in labour. It was her 12th delivery, and ten members of her Māori family were present in the delivery room!

I felt confident about the situation and found Māoris were very friendly, family-minded people, relaxed and accepting of the processes of pregnancy and labour.

The patient's labour was progressing well. The lady's husband and her sister were by her side most of the time, supporting her with encouraging words as the contractions continued in regular strength and frequency. They helped her to change to comfortable positions as she sat on the delivery bed. The remaining family members, who were familiar with the process of birth having been present on other family labours, stood further back, leaning on the walls of the delivery room. The family shared that the mother had 11 girls while her sister had 13 boys and was desperate for a baby girl.

Labour progressed rapidly and another baby girl was successfully delivered. Everyone was thrilled; it was almost a party atmosphere. I worked quickly to dress the 7 lb 2 oz baby girl while the relatives helped wash and dress the mother. Tea and toast for the exhausted mother is a traditional custom after delivery and this was no different.

The new baby was passed around the family to be welcomed, kissed and cuddled. When it was the turn of the mother's sister, she looked longingly at the girl in her arms.

'She is yours, my love,' said the mother to her sister.

The whole family applauded, many crying with joy. I was totally shocked, not knowing what to do about the situation I was witnessing. The following morning, my manager explained to me that Māori people are very loving and family-minded and that, as they have such large families and often live close together, the birth mother would be in contact with her baby. I realised I had learnt more from the Māori mother than the mother ever learnt from me.

23. MAIL BOX FULL

The chilly morning air saw me dash across the car park after my night shift to my waiting Nissan. Freezing, I was relieved the car started first time as I ensured the heater was set to full. However, the car windows were only misty, without the thick ice I was accustomed to in England.

Driving home to Christchurch from Burwood, I met the sun rising over the horizon; it would be fully daylight by the time I reached home. The traffic density was low, the traffic flowing freely as I started to think about the residents whose lives I had tried to improve. They were the original ten-pound Poms who had migrated to New Zealand to give their children a better life. As the children grew up, they flew the nest for reasons of education, employment and marriage. Their parents were now left to care for themselves and, as one partner died or became ill, they were at the mercy of the charities or church. New Zealand was a young country and, although developing fast, it did not have the sophisticated care and support systems found in the western world.

These days my mind just kept playing the same old film of thoughts to me: just what had I done wrong? I had been working to my job description. Only a week before that nasty interview, Neil and Barbara had said my job was safe and they liked all I was doing and how I was doing it. Tom and I had taken out our larger mortgage in the belief our combined salaries would cover it comfortably.

I dragged my mind away from the same old, same old and tried to focus on the only thing that gave me joy these days, Bobbie and Anna. I was pleased to find no sight of Tom as I put the key in the latch, and I took the dogs for a walk before facing the now scary postbox.

I treated myself to an extra-strong pot of coffee before I walked back down for the post. I caught my breath as I pulled out a brown A4 envelope. I instantly recognised the stamp of our solicitors. Bravely ripping it open, I found that he had enclosed a copy of the letter sent to Neil. I was horrified to learn that this letter was a reply to Neil's personal attack on me, which had presented me as an overbearing, disagreeable person who had a hierarchical authoritarian attitude.

Before I could read David's response, I retched. The two-faced Neil had told me, on the day I left, that he regretted my departure and I also recalled all his crocodile tears.

I braced myself for Neil's response.

Dear Sir,

So far as the personal attack on Mrs Lauri is concerned, the image of an overbearing, disagreeable person which the director attempts to create in his letter is totally unrealistic. Our experience of Mrs Lauri, and that of a number of other people to whom we have spoken, is that she has a strong sense of professional responsibility and will be very firm where matters of

nursing practice are concerned but that she is a pleasant and reasonable person.
The real issue in this matter is the standard of care provided in the hospital and geriatric institutions operated by the church council.
When Mrs Lauri became principal nurse, she did a review of nursing practice in the various institutions and found immediately that the standards were disturbingly, even dangerously, low. Patients were not receiving the basic essentials of privacy, decency, cleanliness and proper care.

This was just the first half of his letter but I took a break to fill up my coffee and to collect my thoughts. I felt calmed by David's assertive and honest response. As I dared to read on, I was pleased that David included evidence of all the failings of care provided by the home, directing the complaint away from me. He pointed out that as principal nurse it was my duty to improve the standard of nurse care as quickly as possible.

Reading that letter, I was reassured that of course I had done nothing wrong. He re-emphasised that I had experienced constructive dismissal and that we could avoid litigation if discussions took place.

I felt happier after reading David's soothing letter, although worried about what Tom would think, and I felt relaxed enough to doze on the sun lounger by the pool.

As it turned out, Tom was happy with the letter, so I was happy too and had a few good days. Work, swimming, walking the dogs – life began to feel even pleasurable at times. I still kept an eye on that postbox, and I heard myself groan when my hand withdrew yet another brown envelope. David Mason again reporting the writ had been issued and served on the church. He attached a copy of the statement of claim. He explained that the church had 30 days to file a statement of defence.

The section of the statement of claim which shocked me was the following:

The Plaintiff seeks:
A] A declaration that the Defendant's reputation of the contract of employment was wrongful.
B] Damages of $10.000.00 for loss of income.
C] General damages of £25.000.00.
D] The cost of and incidental to this action.
E] Such further or other relief as the Court thinks just.

I thought I would have preferred an apology, but I knew there was no way that Tom would entertain that idea.

24. THE ONLY WAY IS UP

The antidepressants seemed to be working and I was beginning to think on more constructive lines. I even felt I would like to socialise! Tom showed no interest in accepting any of the invitations which occasionally came our way to dinner, drinks or rugby matches. I decided to enjoy some of the restaurants with colleagues and catch the odd film whenever Tom was away on business. I had to budget carefully as Tom banked my salary each month and asked for a breakdown of my spends. These outings made me remember what fun was, how therapeutic laughs with a group of girls could be. On those occasions I found the old me, I could enjoy a laugh and hearing stories from the lives of the others made me realise how inward-looking I had become. Those nights out were a medicine in themselves.

Tom and I could never manage any minibreaks due to the dogs as we had no boarding for them. In any case, Tom was travelling with work, away from home for two to five days most months, so he did not have much interest in travelling for leisure. He worked for a company called Quick Stick, which manufactured sticky labels for jars, cars, vans and aeroplanes.

Our personal relationship had been platonic at times in our marriage but I did not care, choosing to focus on my work. As early as two years into our marriage, I had spoken to my mother about divorce but she was horrified because I belonged to the generation where divorce was seen as a taboo. She claimed I would disgrace our family by such an action. I was a person who had a very strong sense of family duty and so I accepted the expectations placed on me.

However, all the recent problems had stirred so many emotions. It was as if somebody had sieved the flour and all the dregs, which needed to be broken up, had appeared. I had become more and more conscious of the controlling ways of my husband, although they had always been there. I needed to find a way to break them up.

I began to wonder what the future held for us. Our financial estate was declining. The New Zealand dollar was falling against the pound. Where it was two dollars to the pound when we had arrived, it was now one dollar fifty cents to the pound.

Socialising again, I found clearer thought came to me as I began to see things in perspective – I suppose the company of my new friends was stimulating for my thought processes. I knew for certain that Tom was adamant about the court case and would fight to the bitter end, which I was convinced would leave us bankrupt. The solicitor had already cost us $2,000. Despite the church's continuous pleading of poverty, they were a very wealthy organisation, having been able to afford to engage a top solicitor. The case was to be heard in a high court. I feared their aim was to assassinate my character, which would have destroyed my nursing career. I believed that even if we won there would always be a shadow on my character. I also knew that prejudice was alive and kicking and that my immigrant status would go against me in any court case.

A clearer picture of matters was building in my mind now my confidence was returning; mixing with more people had done me the world of good. Knowing Tom's previous tendency to walk out of jobs if he didn't agree with something, I realised that if I was left as the main breadwinner we would not cover this new mortgage. We were living on a cliff edge. I realistically considered Tom's employment habits: he had held countless jobs over the years, and there had been several spells of unemployment.

The doctor had added diazepam to my existing prescription of antidepressants, and my nursing knowledge warned me that if I did not make some wise choices I could be on the road to addiction. I suddenly knew what we needed to do and what I wanted to do, rather taking myself by surprise.

Tom was about to leave on yet another of his business trips when I somehow found the courage to tell him that I thought we should return to England. I tried to soften the blow by promising that we could live wherever he wanted and I would support him in any career choice he made.

Tom blew a fuse; I had never seen him so mad. He screamed at me to do what I wanted and I knew it was an angry bluff because he thought I would not dare to do what I wanted.

Years of doing what he wanted had finally worn me down and I decided to find the power to break free from his control.

I am surprised that he did not die from the shock when, on his return from his latest sojourn, our house had a 'For sale' sign in the garden. I had researched quarantine for Bobbie and Anna and a very kind gentleman official had helped me to complete the necessary forms for the dogs to travel to England. I had invested in the correct dog travel boxes and I had been building up their cage time each day in preparation for their long-haul flight. Their six-month quarantine had been booked in a Devon kennel. Their flights were booked! I was quite proud of my organisational skills.

Tom had tried the silent treatment on his return, but eventually he couldn't stop himself from enquiring about the house sale. I don't think he could believe the new me who, for once, was in control. It seemed to make him unable to act.

Within six months we found ourselves waiting at Christchurch Airport for the flight to Los Angeles, where we changed for Heathrow. I was very surprised to see a large group of people I had never set eyes on gathered around us saying their farewells to Tom. One man shouted to Tom, as if he was some celebrity, that they had all been following his situation at every stage. I felt bemused. Another man smuggled a card into Tom's hand and I just caught his whisper: 'She was too upset to come herself.' I could only guess it was a farewell card from the girl in his office, who Tom had often spoken of with great fondness. She seemed to be everything I wasn't and he had enthused about her bright clothes, her cheerful demeanour, the animal posters she covered the office walls with. She had sounded like his heroine. I did not care!

I heard Tom regaling them all with the drama – that we had not finished with the legal case against the church and that we would be returning for the court case. Realising how much he had been broadcasting to all and sundry of our personal business, I understood Tom had been the one feeding the press with all the information on the abysmal conditions in the care homes.

25. WELCOME HOME

Arriving back on British soil felt surreal. Our dream had turned into a nightmare from which I was trying to awaken us with this decision to return to Cornwall. I knew we had to organise a new life as soon as possible, to be proactive, so our first action was to purchase a car at the Nissan garage in Bodmin.

We were well known in the area, having lived around here for over a decade so, in some ways, it was nice to see the welcoming smiles of acquaintances, but there were also the nosey questions to face as to the reason for our return. One advantage was that we knew who to trust and where to go for advice and almost overnight we became the owners of a red Nissan Micro and tenants of a flat at Pepper Pot Cottage.

There were even immediate job offers, which were flattering to our egos. However, we did not want to jump from the frying pan into the fire and Tom was hesitant about accepting work at the garage.

My emotions swelled from the warm reception I received at my old nursing headquarters. I couldn't believe it when I set eyes on Miss Rodkin, sat in her office as if she had never moved. Her smile was genuine as she saw me.

'Hello, Sister Lauri, how nice to see you.' Her firm handshake was evidence of her feelings.

THE CATALYST NURSE

'Are you here on holiday? You wouldn't like a job, would you?'

When I said yes there was no hesitancy in her voice.

'Bodmin for you, my girl, we have just lost the nurse there.'

Tom could find no enthusiasm for our new life, even though we had achieved so much in such a short time. Personally, I was delighted to discover that England hadn't changed. *Coronation Street, Emmerdale Farm* and *Panorama* were just a few of the old favourite television programmes still showing. *Desert Island Discs, The Archers* and *Does the Team Think?* were all still being broadcast on the radio.

The nursing office in Bodmin was easily found, situated in a modern building close to the town centre. It felt good to be back in a more formal British setting and to be able to wear a nurse's uniform again with respect and pride. It was pleasurable to find myself in a nicely decorated, ordered environment.

I had to admit to missing the New Zealand sun as we experienced the typical British rainy days and cloudy skies. I particularly missed lazing on a sunbed by the pool, although, due to the circumstances, we had never truly been able to relax and enjoy to the full that beautiful house.

Sister Nadine Blanket, senior nurse, introduced herself to me and I tried to blank out the memories of myself in such a position in my post in New Zealand. Her welcome was enthusiastic and my first name was not used, much to my delight. I was offered a cup of tea – oh how good it was to be back on British soil and to enjoy British customs. A wall of the smiling faces of nurses who recognised me made me feel we had made the right decision to return. I had missed such hearty cheer.

'There's no place like home,' became the answer to be shared whenever anybody enquired about our reasons for returning. People accepted homesickness must have blighted our happiness and I left them to reach their own further conclusions.

I admired the routine, which had been so lacking in New Zealand.

'We meet in the office at 8.30 a.m. for liaison and discussing new cases. You're welcome to join us for lunch from 1 to 2 p.m., or whenever you wish, if your calls are not too far out. Then report in at 5.30 p.m. – this gives us continuity and we can soon be aware if there are any problems.'

This was the way I liked to work: a schedule where everyone knew what was expected of them, and the knowledge that support was at hand and there was somebody overlooking our performance. Good patient care was at the heart of everything.

As I was to work as a midwife, I was told I would be working two to three nights per week but if I was called out in the night, I could start at 10 the following morning. Everything was strictly organised and I was to meet the doctors at the surgery and undertake some orientation calls.

I had missed all this British organisation; I wished Patrick, Barbara and Neil could have been here to witness what good nursing care was based on.

'Monday is always a busy day, so if we can sort out the work early it makes a big difference to finishing time. I would rather start early because you never know what the day may bring. Plus, in the summer the traffic is horrendous and can put an extra hour on your working day. If you have finished your tea, we will make a start.' Sister Blanket was friendly but efficient. I smiled as I thought Neil would have seen her as another Mrs Thatcher.

Obviously there were going to be some similarities with the New Zealand deficiencies, as human nature is the same everywhere, and I met some grumpy members of staff. The senior GP, Dr Bradly, was bad-tempered to the point of rudeness, and I sensed no one liked him. I heard the story of the previous year when at retirement age he gave notice to his partners he was leaving. A party was arranged and all gave generous donations to his leaving gift as the relief was so great. On the night of the leaving party all was going well, although the feeling of optimism among staff about the appointment of a new and more social and progressive GP was hidden from Dr Bradly. Finally, in his reply to the speeches given by his partners, Dr Bradly said, 'I didn't realise just how much we meant to each other, I can't possibly leave now!' Perhaps I should have given such a speech to Neil, Barbara and Patrick.

Then, of course, we had the usual bulldog of a medical receptionist who people warned me of. One woman cautioned: 'This lady takes a lot on herself. When you leave a message for the doctor with her, for example, if you want to catheterise a patient, you will discover that the message may never reach the doctor, and she will give you the answer. If a patient has asked for some antibiotics, she may decide to do the prescription. Doctors are busy, they don't always look at what is on the prescription and just sign it. One nurse wrote a prescription out for gin and tonic and the GP signed it without noticing.'

The warning of that woman reminded me of all the medication sagas I had dealt with in New Zealand. I hoped that there were not going to be many more of these unprofessional tales.

What a wonderful sight greeted me on my return to Pepper Pot Cottage – my two welcoming bundles of fur. I was truly over the moon, as were they. They might need a good groom but they had survived and, most importantly, had not forgotten their mum!

The first day, working alone, found me eager even though I was aware that they always gave new nurses the difficult patients. I was ready for the challenge of Bodmin Moor on this cold, wet and misty day. I had my directions on how to get to the Pully farmhouse and the nursing care required by the elderly lady living there. The building was dilapidated and the scruffy house was a sight to behold, but my eyes were diverted by a young man in his 20s standing in front of me, stark naked. He told me I was late! He stood aside to allow me to enter, informing me his ill mother was up the stairs in the first room I would come to. I ran up the stairs with their threadbare carpet. The single light bulb was dim, revealing walls and furnishings in great need of repair. Inside the room, I found a frail lady in her late 80s lying in a bed between worn grey sheets and a crochet blanket. The lady was pleased to see me, cooperative, and spent most of her time telling me how good her son was to her. Having completed my tasks, I collected my things and headed for the stairs.

'Do you want a coffee?' the naked son asked as he stood with his hand on the banister at the bottom of the stairs.

'No thank you, I am running late, so I must go.' I dashed past the man, then through a hole in the wall. I cursed as I tried to unlock the car door; I had forgotten the rule – you never lock your car door when you think the patient may be difficult so you can make a quick getaway. After the uneventful remainder of the day, I arrived at the nurses office to find Sister Blanket waiting for me with a quizzical look. I related the visit to Pully Farm and suggested it would have been helpful to have had prior warning.

'We will see how you get on in Berryfields,' was the only comment made before she turned to leave the office and go home. I felt a bit worried, my anxieties still just below the surface. Surely this was not going to be full of misunderstandings like my New Zealand experience. However, I also understood this was just the abrupt manner of a good sister who had to run a tight ship with no room for emotion; a strong backbone was expected of British nurses and I would soon slot back into that system which I respected.

Parking my car on the shingle in front of Pepper Pot Cottage that evening, I could clearly see Tom pacing up and down the long lounge. I wondered what had made him so anxious.

I knew he was irate over something from the way he was acting. Seeing the brown A4 envelope, I guessed at the reason for his frustration. It was not a good sign when I spotted Bobbie and Anna hiding together behind the sofa.

'We've had a letter at long last.' Tom almost threw the envelope at me.

The letter from David Mason read:

Further to my telephone conversation with you, I have now had discussions with the solicitor representing the church regarding settlement. I have put to him the proposal I discussed with you in May, that the church give you an apology together with an acknowledgement of your professional competence and that unfair pressure was put on you to resign. I have also sought payment by them of your legal costs. Their solicitor seemed to think that the first part might be acceptable but had doubts about payment of costs. I have told him those are my instructions from you and that it is a package to be accepted or rejected. I have also stressed to him your preparedness to return to New Zealand for a hearing of the matter. As soon as I have a response to that formal offer, I will let you know what it is.

In the meanwhile, I must record my views regarding the letter your husband sent to the bishop. The bishop found the letter thoroughly offensive and the fact that it has been written has cast a rather dark shadow over my discussions with their solicitor. It has made my task very much harder. Although I am prepared to accept that your husband was motivated by concern for you, I must make it absolutely clear to you both that Mr Lauri's letter has only done harm to your case. Any repartition of that sort of action will make my position untenable.

THE CATALYST NURSE

I trust you have been able to settle back into a comfortable life in England. I will report to you again as and when there are further developments.

*Yours faithfully,
David Mason*

Something in me shattered. Tom had opened my post; Tom had interfered in my business without telling me about writing to the bishop; Tom had made a right mess and now he was angry. I should be the angry one. Just what did he think he was doing by such an action? He was a madman. But then hadn't I always known that? All my happiness at returning to England evaporated. The despair of New Zealand was still haunting us. I could stand his scheming, cunning and interfering ways no longer. I was dumbfounded. People react differently under stress but did I really know Tom? Yes, he wanted to help me, but surely he realised this was not the way to do it. I sat, almost unable to move, in weary incomprehension at the dinner table. Nothing surprised me, so I did not bat an eyelid when Tom announced he had already replied.

I did not wish to see what on earth he had written but he pushed his efforts at a reply across the table for me to read.

Dear Mr Mason,

We are in receipt of your letter of 13th October 1986, the first one, incidentally, we have received from you since our return to the UK, and we are rather disappointed to have had no earlier response.

Mr Lauri's only regret in sending his letter of 19th August 1986 to the bishop (purely out of frustration at not hearing from you) is his lies and hypocrisy of the church.

I truly thought that there would have been a few quiet words with the committee, who would realise the error of their ways and come to some kind of agreement. Mrs Lauri was away at the time and when she phoned you, I thought you would have some good news for her.

We are sorry if the bishop found Mr Lauri's letter thoroughly offensive. If anything was thoroughly offensive and libellous it was the letter of Neil, the director, of 25th September 1984.

If the bishop finds thoroughly offensive the fact that he ruined the career, health and life of Mrs Lauri, so do we.

If he finds thoroughly offensive those who died under suspicious circumstances and drug abuse, so do we.

If he finds thoroughly offensive the mismanagement of such a high-ranking and professional person, so do we. If he finds thoroughly offensive the lies printed in Action magazine, so do we.

The fact that he has turned two Christians away from Christianity is appalling.

The church are guilty of disinformation and lies. We are appalled that they pursue such unsubstantiated allegations and that they, supposedly of superior standards, should have sunk to those depths.

They have oppressed and intimidated us through three years of hell, caused great embarrassment and jeopardised both our *careers. They have been incredibly arrogant and should publicly apologise, unreservedly, for the distress and damage caused. Their actions were so disgraceful and deplorable we cannot see how they can fail to be disciplined and if those involved were men of honour, they would resign.*

We look forward to your letter of their response to our formal offer, but must express our feelings about the unfair and lax treatment, which we find pertinacious. We would be pleased to receive copies of letters apparently sent but not received since last May and would request a monthly update of proceedings in future.

Yours faithfully,
Tom Lauri

As I had come to expect, Tom had requested no input from me. I thought he made some good points in his letter but there was also much I totally disagreed with – mainly his tone and manner, which was, in my opinion, unprofessional, argumentative and, of course, disrespectful. My exhaustion had returned but I managed to pull myself together, somehow, to face work the next day.

Sat in the Bodmin nurses office, reading through the day's calls, I noticed one with an address on the Berryfield Estate. As I approached the street on the Berryfields Estate, which had been easy to find, I discovered that the house numbers were obscure. Eventually, finding the right house and ringing the bell, I found myself confronted by a very large, unshaven, heavily tattooed man in his 30s. He wore a black tracksuit, which, due to his rather prominent beer belly, didn't meet in the middle, giving him a tyre of overhanging fatty tissue between the top and bottom. After a sleepless night, I felt physically sick at such a sight.

I introduced myself and he opened the door wider, indicating by a movement of his head that I should enter the house. The patient, a woman in her 70s, looked towards me with a puffy, wrinkled red face. Sitting in an easy chair by a roaring log fire, she held her left leg straight out in front of her with the dressing removed, clearly revealing a large suppurating leg ulcer on her shin.

'Will you take off your dripping coat and put the bag down, nurse, me bloods getting on the furniture,' the woman howled. There appeared no room for sociability in this house. Finishing the task, I turned to pick up my dressing bag, which had been placed on the dinning chair behind her. The bag was not there.

'What happened to my bag?' I asked politely.

'Ain't seen no bag,' said the woman gruffly.

The internal door flew open and the tattooed man appeared in the doorway. I asked him about my bag. He replied, looking at his mother for confirmation, 'She never brought a bag in with her.' Once again, I asked if I could have the bag I had definitely brought in with me. It was full of dressings, some of which were used on his mother's leg, so I obviously did have it when I arrived at the house. They played out this little charade for a few more minutes before the internal door opened slowly and a woman, roughly the same age as the tattooed man, waddled in and aggressively stared at me. Yet again, feeling incredibly annoyed, I repeated my request for the dressing bag I had brought in with me. I was assertive in my manner and, feeling increasingly angry, now stood very straight with my shoulders back, my feet slightly apart. Being a good size 16, I was not about to be pushed over. A thought flashed across my mind: how come I could not be so assertive against my own husband's menacing behaviour? Magically the bag was found! I had that strong backbone that Sister Blanket required.

My time had been more than wasted and I had much to catch up on so I dashed out. Throwing the bag into the passenger seat and cursing at the persistent rain, I turned the ignition key to start the car. The engine turned over but there was no movement. After several attempts I decided to check the outside of the car. The wheels were missing and the car was balancing on bricks. I could not think how I had not noticed, even in my hurry. I guess I was still blinded by the fury from my recent encounter. I used words I didn't know I knew. There was nothing else to do but go to the police station, so, after locking up the vehicle, I made my way there in the still drizzling rain. I glanced back at the house but nobody was in view – they had probably moved on to their next crime!

'You had your car wheels taken when you parked outside a house in Berryfields!' the police officer exclaimed in a broad Cornish accent. 'Well, my dear, I think you were brave to even attempt to park in Berryfields. Even the police don't do that.' He continued looking for some paper, presumably to make notes, his eyes sparkling as though he was trying to conceal his laughter. A patrol officer took me to the local garage and explained the situation to the mechanics, who also had a bit of a laugh before they set out to find my car and replace the wheels. I did hope they would have a set available.

Somehow the incident reminded me of the highway patrol incident in New Zealand when I had been the subject of laughter.

26. THE FULL STOP

Placing my wet coat and shoes on the radiator, hoping they would dry by the morning, I felt something dying inside me – this wasn't the Cornwall I remembered. Had we made a terrible mistake? I had a sense of déjà vu, the feelings were so similar to the ones I experienced in New Zealand. I felt that we were on another treadmill of disaster.

Tom was becoming even more sarcastic and vitriolic towards me. Even Bobbie and Anna seemed unhappy and I realised they were not getting as much exercise as when we had lived in New Zealand, where the weather enticed us out for long walks in the park. I suppose the climate change was a huge shock to their bodies, as they had been raised in such a different weather system.

Tom's behaviour overwhelmed me. My inner voice instructed me to relax, not to allow him to see I was upset. To do so would just give the bully more power. He was trying to achieve more control. I would lower my shoulders, relax, take deep breaths and distract myself with whatever tasks I could. He had developed many techniques to exercise his control, and I would see his reflection in the window in front of me as he leant on the wall by the door, just standing with his arms crossed and staring at me from behind. I can still feel the eyes boring into my back, which caused me to shudder. I felt cold and wanted to run from the room but I had to tell myself to keep calm, that things would only get worse if he saw me flinch.

The tactics had changed over the years; not only did I receive the silent treatment I had grown accustomed to, but he started staring, sighing, obstructing my path – all at random moments. He started abusing me via music.

After a full day at work, I would sit at the computer on my desk in the upstairs office, which I had created in a small bedroom. When I needed full concentration to write up the notes on my patients or to research patients' complaints, the music would start. He had fitted a music centre in the lounge, which would spring into life. His favourite music from the 1960s would deafen me as he played it at full volume, the same songs over and over again. Tom knew which songs I did not like and he would play those. I tried to reason with him, tried to explain the financial advantages we would gain if I performed well and that I couldn't do that if I could not concentrate. However, my pleas fell on stony ground. I would stuff cotton wool in my ears and wear a woolly hat to cut out the noise, but concentration was still difficult and I found it hard to carry on. I did try going to bed early then working in the night but Tom soon realised what I was up to. The electric power was cut off before he went to bed to prevent my plan.

As I moved around the kitchen from one point to another, I could see his eyes searching every part of my body, his mouth twisted into a sneering expression. A deep sigh escaped his lips as I passed by him into the hallway en route to the lounge. All of his behaviour had become unbearable.

THE CATALYST NURSE

Tom had left a letter he had written open on the bed, I guess with the intention of me finding it.

Dear David Mason,

Your letter to Mrs Lauri of 14th September 1987 was duly received, contents noted, and forwarded to our local solicitor, who is taking an increasing interest in our case, advisory only at the moment.
Why did you find my letter of 9th July 1987 offensive? What kind of letter do you expect to receive after ignoring us for 18 months, ignoring three letters from Mrs Lauri and a previous one from myself?
We note from your letter that there is no possibility of settlement due to my letter to the bishop of August 1986, that my letter was offensive and unreasonable.
I stand by every word of that letter, and look forward to it being read out in court, or printed in the press. Perhaps then we may get some answers.
As Mrs Lauri commented in her letter January 1986, we are sorry if the bishop found my letter thoroughly offensive. If anything is thoroughly offensive and libellous it was the director's letter of 25th September 1984.
If the bishop finds thoroughly offensive the fact that he ruined the career, health and life of Mrs Lauri, so do we. If he finds thoroughly offensive the fact that people died under suspicious circumstances and from drug abuse while in their care, so do we. If he finds thoroughly offensive lies printed in his Action

magazine, so do we. If he finds thoroughly offensive the fact he has turned two Christians away from Christianity, so do we.
Mrs Lauri also commented on your laxity at the time but apparently to no avail. I will not be used as your scapegoat in this case. Please draw the attention of Mrs Lauri's letter of January 1986 to the church.
You know of our formal complaint about this case and our feelings about your conduct.
We now require specific answers for which we shall allow you a reasonable time to reply but please be clear should a satisfactory reply not be received we shall refer the matter to the New Zealand District Law Society.
The care given by the church was despicable and an affront to civilised values.

Tom continued his unprofessional rant with a series of questions in the letter.

Why did you not reply to Mrs Lauri's letters of 12th January, 4th March, 11th April and my letters of 12th May and 9th July?
Why are the only two letters you have sent been received only after I had written to the bishop?
Why have you ignored my claim, dated 12th May, against the church?
Why did you not notify us, your clients, of your change of address? Why have you not demanded replies to your letters from the church?
Why have we not received copies of letters of correspondence which you verbally said by phone you had sent?

THE CATALYST NURSE

I wanted to scream at Tom, telling him that he had dug a deeper hole for us through his actions. I wanted to cut ourselves free from all of this and let it slide into the past. It was now ruining any future we hoped to have. I had done all I could for those poor souls but now it was time to think about our health and the state of our 30-year marriage, which was being destroyed by this insanity. I knew Tom did care but he needed to let go of this nonsense now; it was like a lead weight taking us all down.

I tried to study Tom when he was not watching me. He must have been suffering from depression and apathy, I was sure. Six months had passed and he showed no interest in finding work despite having received some job offers. I knew he mourned the loss of our New Zealand home and pool, the banter of his workmates, maybe a certain young lady, the climate. I also knew that he felt, like me, a sense of desolation at the way we had messed up our lives. The standard of our English accommodation was so much inferior to what we had been able to own out there.

Therefore it was a huge relief one night to return to find a smile on Tom's face. He was his old enthusiastic self as he explained that he had found a franchise he believed would be lucrative, selling batteries, torches and videos.

Desperate for happiness in our lives, I offered Tom my full support. I was happy to accept yet another relocation; we weren't happy here so I was enthusiastic to give anything a go. Apparently we would need to move to West Sussex as he also needed to cover the Isle of Wight. I offered to look for nursing vacancies in those areas, desperate to bring joy back into our lives.

It was refreshing to see the return of Tom's zest for life. Even Bobbie and Anna seemed to pick up on his mood, their tails wagging much more frequently. Maybe they were recovering from the stress of the long journey and life in quarantine.

Tom had done his homework, even finding a new housing estate near Worthing. I dared to feel excited once more. Tom had even got a date fixed with the leader of the franchise for a Devon meeting.

However, my heart fell when he spoilt everything by adding, 'While I'm there, I will call and see a publisher I used to deal with. If we can't get anywhere with this solicitor then we'll write about it. I want you to talk to him, if he's interested.'

I dared to hope this would be another one of his crazy ideas, but the danger was that Tom usually put his ideas into fruition and it wasn't long until we found ourselves in the office of David James Publishers. The publisher was skilled at interviewing and my initial hesitation evaporated as he put me at ease and my story began to flow from my lips. I discovered it was rather therapeutic sharing everything that had gone on, and felt reassured by the nodding head of this sympathetic man who kept encouraging me to tell him more as he plied us with tea and cakes.

I was impressed by his honesty as he explained that he was not out just to gain financially from us. He offered genuine, caring advice. His words contained warnings: 'If you write your story, you must remember these points. You could probably never work as a registered nurse again. You would have the New Zealand Health Authority enquiring about it; remember, they have been lax and would not want to be seen in a bad light. The church would certainly have a lot to say as they probably hold a lot of sway in Christchurch. They would be concerned about a loss in donations to the church.'

He made the suggestion that I should wait until I retired, whenever that would be, and then write my book as a fictional work, changing the names of the people involved.

As you slot the final piece into this jigsaw of my story you will realise that I took his words on board to give you a clearer understanding of my title, *The Catalyst Nurse*.

The house in Aingmering that we bought upon return from New Zealand.

EPILOGUE

My hope is that my story will inspire others and help them to realise that success means embarking on the journey, holding on to one's principles, even if the destination ends up a surprise. I persevered on my rocky journey to improve the life of the residents in my care, and I believe my discontent with the standards I met was indeed the catalyst for change and that I did bring a better quality of life into the world of the forgotten Poms. We sow many seeds on our journey through life and we do not always see the fruit ourselves.

As you will have observed, my husband was a salesman, trained by his profession to achieve monetary goals. It was a constant battle to match our personalities, which were polar opposites, to find an agreed path and I often ended up treading his route because I was a peace-lover. I could and would speak my mind in my professional role – in fact, I was known for doing so quite strongly – but living with a manipulative partner, exposed to his gaslighting techniques over many years, often robbed me of clarity of thought and independence of mind within my home life. Thirty years of marriage are hard to dismiss and I must point out there were some happy moments. Tom did have my interests at heart and was concerned for the Pom residents, but his mind always focussed on budgets and he lost sight, I believe, of what really matters in life: empathy, compassion and love of our neighbour.

You also now know that on my return to Cornwall, I immediately found another district nursing sister and midwife job, but I never got promoted above that; I was given responsibility but I felt I always had a blot on my records. I spent the last 16 years of my career working in Worthing. However, I can rest in my retirement knowing that, despite everything, I've had a good and fulfilling career and have enjoyed the various challenges life has thrown at me. I believe many have benefitted from my nursing skills and dedication to my patients. The Nightingale Pledge was always at the forefront of my heart and mind and I based all my actions on the nursing ethics of autonomy, beneficence, justice and non-maleficence.

There is no doubt that the fallout from the church homes in New Zealand affected our marriage, and I went home one day to find the house empty. Tom had left me three uniforms: white for midwifery, navy for general and striped for Marie Curie. His practical mind had left me a cup, saucer, plate, knife and fork. We had not spoken properly in the previous five years; we used to communicate through the dogs. Due to Tom's silent approach, it was difficult to discuss anything. I eventually approached a solicitor who wrote to Tom asking about his feelings. He said he did not love me but could not see why he should leave the house. However, in the divorce, which took a lengthy four years because of his refusal to respond to letters or attend court, I took the house because I could afford to pay the mortgage and he couldn't.

THE CATALYST NURSE

My new independence was good for me, as I was able to heal from the years of mental abuse. I was on my own for five years and then met a most generous and caring man who I married and then nursed as he battled prostate cancer. Alone again for a further seven years, I confided in an Italian nursing colleague that it would be lovely to meet a man to take me out for lunch! What a charming phone call I received from her neighbour who said, 'I'd like to take a lady out for lunch.'

I found my soulmate and, for those who believe in karma, I feel my well-meant intentions throughout my life have blessed me now with the peace and happiness I never knew in my first marriage. I have nothing but appreciation for the love of my wonderful third husband.

I had given my soul to the church establishments in which I worked, not to the church itself but to the patients I had vowed to help. I left New Zealand as an empty vessel but, over the years, I have been blessed to hear that my actions ignited change and even Patrick apparently confided, 'I think she was right.'

Time returned my strength and my faith survived. I had sacrificed so much personally as I fought the battle but blessings have been bestowed upon me as I now enjoy a very comfortable life with the ability to travel and explore the world via my love of cruising. My loyal husband is my best friend and rock who has patiently encouraged me, together with my nephew, Richard, to write this book to share with you my message: persevere with integrity in the vocation to which you have been called, knowing that you will be making a difference to the lives of others, even if you never see the results yourself.

Keith and I.

Printed in Great Britain
by Amazon